Imperium Press was founded in 2018 to supply students and laymen with works in the history of rightist thought. If these works are available at all in modern editions, they are rarely ever available in editions that place them where they belong: outside the liberal weltanschauung. Imperium Press' mission is to provide right thinkers with authoritative editions of the works that make up their own canon. These editions include introductions and commentary which place these canonical works squarely within the context of tradition, reaction, and counter-Enlightenment thought—the only context in which they can be properly understood.

Gaetano Mosca (1858–1941) was an Italian jurist, political theorist, senator, and influential figure in the development of elite theory. Educated in law at the University of Palermo, he taught constitutional law at Palermo, Rome, and Turin, and was appointed senator for life in 1919. Mosca is best known for his *Elementi di Scienza Politica* (1896), in which he argued that all societies are governed by a cohesive ruling minority—a concept that helped define modern political realism. Beyond theory, Mosca engaged directly with Italian politics and society, especially in Sicily, where he was born. His essays *What Is the Mafia?* (1901) and the collection *Men and Things of Sicily* (1902–1933) analyse the island's informal power structures and serve as empirical case studies of para-sovereignty. These works grounded his broader theory in lived observation and remain essential for understanding how legitimacy and rule persist even in the absence of effective state authority.

WHAT IS THE MAFIA?

GAETANO MOSCA

Translated by
THOMAS NICHOLLS

Introduction by
EDWARD MAXWELL III

PERTH
IMPERIUM PRESS
2025

Published by Imperium Press

www.imperiumpress.org

Cosa è la Mafia
Published in *Giornale degli Economisti*, Luglio 1901

FIRST EDITION

A catalogue record for this book is available from the National Library of Australia

ISBN 978-1-923104-95-2 Paperback
ISBN 978-1-923104-96-9 Hardcover
ISBN 978-1-923104-97-6 E-book

Contents

Introduction

Power Beyond Law: Gaetano Mosca on the Mafia and Informal Sovereignty

I. Preliminary

This volume brings together two of the most important texts on Sicilian political life: *What Is the Mafia?* (1900) and selected essays from *Men and Things of Sicily* (1902–1933), here translated into English for the first time. Together, they introduce Gaetano Mosca (1858–1941)—jurist, senator, political theorist, and Sicilian native—at his most empirical and conceptually sharp.

Despite Mosca's influence on elite theory and political sociology, these early works have rarely appeared in English. They deserve attention not as historical curiosities but as contributions to political realism. In an age of institutional decay and rising parallel systems of authority, Mosca's Sicilian writings offer tools for understanding how power persists beyond legality.

The two texts complement one another: theory and observation, centre and periphery. Both converge on a central point—political order rests not on law, but on structure, and where structure fails, informal systems take hold. This introductory essay pursues three goals: to place *What Is the Mafia?* and *Men and Things of Sicily* in their original historical moment; to trace their role in Gaetano Mosca's political thought; and to recover their relevance as tools for analysing political disorder, both past and future.

Mosca wrote these works in the early years of the 20th century,[1] a period of national instability in Italy. Though often treated as peripheral, Sicily functioned as a political laboratory. For Mosca, it provided direct experience with informal power, elite mediation, and communal authority. These shaped not only his early journalism but also his later theory of ruling elites. Unlike the abstract *Ruling Class* (1896), the works collected here engage directly with municipal budgets, riots, vendettas, and clientelist networks.

In *Men and Things of Sicily*, Mosca defines the mafia thus:

> Sicilians use the word in two different, though related, senses: first, to denote an attitude that, until recently, was widespread among certain classes in Sicily; and second, to refer to a number of small criminal associations.
>
> The term "mafia" describes the attitude of those who believe that turning to the established authorities in cases of persecution by private enemies shows weakness of character and almost cowardice.[2]

Mosca's key insight lies in rejecting the view of the mafia as a criminal anomaly. He treats it as a sociopolitical structure—an adaptive response to weak sovereignty. Mosca sees it as a symptom of the corruption of a healthy order, but more

1 *Cosa è la Mafia* was delivered as a lecture in Milan in 1900, published in *Giornale degli Economisti* in 1901. *Uomini e cose di Sicilia* was published in 1980, by Sellerio editore, Palermo, but the texts were published earlier in various forms—these bibliographic references have been collected in an appendix of the present volume.

2 "Mafia." In *Encyclopaedia of the Social Sciences*, edited by Edwin R. A. Seligman and Alvin Johnson, vol. 10, 1933.

importantly, as a parallel system of rule, emerging where the state lacks legitimacy and reach.

In cities like London, Paris, and Los Angeles, extra-legal zones operate under euphemisms like "community-led governance."[3] In parts of Europe and the Americas, state presence has become more symbolic than functional. In the U.S., informal enforcement and political violence increasingly blur with official order. Each reflects Mosca's insight—where law is weak, structure returns in new forms.

Mosca's work thus reads as early warning. His mafia emerged not from criminal excess but from institutional failure. Today's West faces similar decay—ideological fracture, elite stagnation, and loss of civic trust. The old moral and legal consensus no longer binds societies together. The cultural logic Mosca described—honour, loyalty, silence—now reappears in tribalism, digital vigilantism, and dissident politics.

These texts offer more than historical insight. They chart the anatomy of a political deterioration—how order persists after legitimacy fades. Mosca's Sicily becomes a lens for the future: not a descent into chaos, but into layered systems of parallel authority.

II. Gaetano Mosca in Historical and Intellectual Context

Biographical Overview and Career Highlights

3 A striking example occurred in Seattle during June 2020, when activists established the Capitol Hill Organized Protest (CHOP, formerly CHAZ). Many outlets praised it as a form of "community-led governance," free from police control—Time magazine even noted that activists "declared the space community-led and free from police" as part of a self-governing "utopia". https://time.com/5851774/seattle-police-capitol-hill-autonomous-zone/.

Gaetano Mosca did not theorise power from afar; he operated within Italy's evolving state machinery—as journalist, professor, senator, and editor. His intellectual clarity came not from detached contemplation, but from proximity to the very elite structures he analysed.

He began his journalistic career in the late 1890s, contributing to *La Tribuna di Roma* (c. 1897) and then to the *Corriere della Sera* from 1901–1925. His early columns dissected the theatrical politics and administrative dysfunction of southern Italy, particularly in writing for the Palermo newspaper *Giornale di Sicilia*.[4]

In academia, Mosca rose quickly. After earning his law degree at Palermo (1881), he taught constitutional law at the University of Palermo (1885–88), then at the University of Rome (1888–96), and finally at the University of Turin (1896–1908). During this period he refined the ideas that appeared in his *Elementi di scienza politica*, first printed at the Camera dei deputati in October 1895 and published in Turin in 1896, where he argued that all societies function through organised ruling minorities. Mosca was made a senator for life by King Victor Emmanuel III in January 1919, becoming an influential voice on reform, education, and civil order. In his Senate speeches he consistently championed procedural stability and warned against moralistic or utopian policies.

In 1901 Mosca published his seminal lecture *What Is the Mafia?* in *Nuova Antologia* (the *Giornale degli Economisti*, July 1901), dissecting Sicily's para-sovereign power structures. Through these essays he helped steer conservative-liberal discourse toward empirical analysis and away from ideological posturing. Although he never joined the Fascist

4 "Gaetano Mosca." *NillAlienum*. Accessed May 17, 2025. https://www.nilalienum.com/gramsci/MoscaG.html.

party, Mosca continued to publish and lecture during the regime. His major works all predate 1922 and consistently favour constitutional order over personal charisma; even in his later engagements he maintained a tone of detached realism.

His embedded position gives *What Is the Mafia?* and *Men and Things of Sicily* their distinctive depth. He wrote not as an outsider, but as a participant-analyst—a dual stance that lends his work lasting authority.

To grasp the urgency of Mosca's work, we must place it within the late liberal era of the Italian kingdom—an age of institutional fragility, ideological fatigue, and uneven national integration. Between the 1870s and 1920s, Italy operated as a constitutional monarchy, but its liberalism remained brittle, its authority symbolic, and its governance deeply fragmented.

The Risorgimento had unified Italy in law but not in substance. The industrialised North uneasily yoked the rural South, where Bourbon legacies, clientelism, and distrust of the state endured. Sicily exemplified this gap. It resisted central norms not through rebellion, but through structured non-compliance—mafioso governance, honour codes, and silent hierarchies.

The liberal state, focused on appearances, proved both overreaching and ineffective. It passed reforms, held elections, and celebrated its own legality—while depending on informal networks and local power brokers to function.[5] Mosca exposed this contradiction: institutions that mimicked legality but ignored law; political offices used as clan tools; justice reduced to mere gesture. By the 1880s, the

5 Davis, John A. *Conflict and Control: Law and Order in Nineteenth-Century Italy*. London: Red Globe Press, 1988. https://doi.org/10.1007/978-1-349-19277-9.

liberal ideals of the Risorgimento had eroded. Corruption, elite deal-making, and rural uprisings exposed the state's shallow roots, especially in the South. The 1893–94 Fasci revolt—and its brutal suppression—shattered any illusion of national cohesion.

As socialism and syndicalism waxed, the liberal regime waned. Mosca warned that without structural realism, parliamentary order would fail. He did not call for dictatorship—but he doubted that liberalism could survive without grounding itself in real power relations. The March on Rome in 1922 confirmed his fears. Liberal Italy collapsed not for lack of ideals, but for failing to understand how power actually operated. Mosca's writings from this era—including his work on Sicily—read as dispatches from a failing state.

Mosca's Contribution to Political Theory

Mosca's most lasting insight lies in his theory of the *classe politica*—the ruling class. First articulated in *Elementi di Scienza Politica* (1896), this doctrine holds that all societies, regardless of form, are governed by an organised minority. The elite may shift—aristocratic, clerical, military, ideological—but its structural dominance remains.

At its core, Mosca's thesis asserts that mass rule is illusory. Though modern regimes claim legitimacy through elections or parliaments, real decisions fall to a small group that controls discourse and asserts its power. This elite must adapt to survive, but it never disappears. The masses remain spectators, occasionally mobilised but structurally excluded.

Mosca broke from idealists like Rousseau and Marx by treating elite rule as a permanent feature of social life. His realism did not imply stagnation though—he argued that regimes fail because elites close ranks, harden ideologically, and sever ties with broader society. He foresaw today's concerns over bureaucratic drift, elite isolation, and waning civic trust. For Mosca, liberalism requires not mass rule, but mechanisms for peaceful elite rotation.

His originality lay in shifting focus from ideals to structure. Constitutions conceal the reality of elite dominance, and behind parliamentary forms lie invisible hierarchies and carefully staged legitimacy. Power, in his model, hides beneath symbols, procedures, and illusion. This theory gave rise to modern elite thought—echoed in Pareto's circulation of elites, Michels's iron law of oligarchy, and Schumpeter's democratic elitism. Yet Mosca stood apart as somewhat of a moderate. Less deterministic than Pareto, less apocalyptic than Michels, he viewed elite rule as inevitable but reformable.

The ruling class thesis also shaped his analysis of the mafia. In Mosca's view, the mafia operated as a subnational ruling class: it enforced norms, resolved disputes, and commanded obedience without legal sanction. Sicily gave him a model of elite power stripped of institutional disguise—authority in its rawest form.

Mosca's political thought directly challenges the myths underpinning democratic ideology. He did not simply criticise democratic dysfunction—he exposed the structural illusions behind claims of popular sovereignty, equal participation, and diffused power. In every regime, cohesive and self-reproducing elites govern, regardless of formal institutions. Universal suffrage, public opinion, and representative government, he warned, often reinforce elite control by masking it.[6] Elections create the impression of mass influence, while candidate selection, media framing, and bureaucratic processes narrow real choices. His theory did not dismiss the public, but recognised the asymmetry

6 Maurice A. Finocchiaro, *Beyond Right and Left: Democratic Elitism in Mosca and Gramsci* (New Haven: Yale University Press, 1999), 146.

between mass disorganisation and elite cohesion. Without structures that enforce elite accountability and renewal, democracy becomes performance—rule by a minority cloaked in majority rhetoric. Mosca viewed parliaments as elite negotiation chambers, not as tools of popular will.[7]

By focusing on elite organisation, Mosca built a non-ideological theory of power. He rejected liberal hopes of the end of hierarchy and Marxist faith in class dissolution. All systems generate elites; political science must study how they form, function, and endure. In today's world of technocracy, oligarchy, and polarisation, Mosca's clarity cuts through populist delusions. His theory offers little comfort—but it reveals power in its true form, preparing us to understand the world as it operates, not as it claims to.

Continuity Between His Theoretical Work and His Sicilian Observations

Sicily provided the raw material for many of Mosca's core insights. Long before he formalised elite theory, Sicilian society appeared before him as a political laboratory, where the absence of effective statehood made the mechanics of power starkly visible. Elections served patronage; mayors acted as local bosses; justice flowed from reputation and retribution, not courts. These patterns did not signal backwardness—they revealed alternative systems of hierarchy, consent, and control. The essays in *Men and Things of Sicily* document these dynamics in sharp detail. Mosca tracks how local prestige forms, how riots express more than hunger, and how unofficial actors resolve disputes. The mafiosi, landowners, and officials he describes function as a parallel

7 Gaetano Mosca. "Teorica dei governi e governo parlamentare." In *Scritti politici di Gaetano Mosca*, vol. I, edited by Giuseppe Sola, 1–60. Turin: UTET, 1968.

elite with their own norms and procedures.

This grounded observation fed directly into *Elementi di Scienza Politica*. His theory of permanent elite rule did not emerge from abstraction—it grew from watching liberal institutions coexist with deeply entrenched informal structures. In *What Is the Mafia?*, the mafia appears as a substitute institution, replicating state functions where formal legitimacy fails.

> The local syndicate not only refrained from causing [the nobleman] any harm but also actively prevented others from doing so, offering a kind of preventive policing that was arguably more effective than the legal system.[8]

Sicily remained Mosca's analytical touchstone. It taught him that rule depends less on law than on social arrangements that compel obedience. In the absence of legal coherence, other structures arise—clientelism, honour, coercion—all capable of sustaining order. To read Mosca on Sicily is to witness his theory in formation. These essays show a thinker drawing from lived reality, where power reveals itself without disguise, and where governance occurs not through rights, but through force, trust, and fear.

III. Sicily as Political Microcosm

Sicilian Exceptionalism and Its Political Ecology

Sicily's political ecology reflects centuries of marginality and foreign rule. From Greek settlers to Bourbon monarchs, the island has lived under distant powers—governed more often than governing. This legacy shaped a culture of scepticism toward central authority and fostered local forms of

8 p. 23.

mediation rooted in kinship, obligation, and personal trust. Where central rule proved exploitative and erratic, Sicilians turned to parallel systems—clans, patrons, mafiosi—that offered protection and dispute resolution. Sicilian mistrust of the state emerged rationally from a history of broken promises and exploitation. Unification deepened this mistrust, as the new Italian state—*de jure* present but *de facto* absent—failed to deliver justice. Legitimacy passed instead to those with local power: priests, bosses, elders.

Sicily's political structure emerged from a long history of foreign rule. Over two millennia, the island fell under successive regimes—Greek, Roman, Arab, Norman, Spanish, Bourbon—each imposing new laws, languages, and exploitative systems without integrating with the local population in any permanent way.

Three regimes left especially lasting marks. The Normans established a feudal template of hereditary privilege and local militarisation, empowering baronial families who ruled with near autonomy. The Spanish Habsburgs ruled through distant viceroys, relying on nobles and clergy while masking administrative weakness with a rigid legalistic approach. Justice became symbolic, inaccessible, and easily bypassed—and corruption flourished. Under the Bourbons, governance stagnated. Repression and surveillance increased, and officials, seen as foreign occupiers, inspired apathy more than open revolt. The population turned inward, seeking protection not from the state but from landowners, clergy, or mafiosi—figures who could mediate and shield against arbitrary authority.

The legacy of these foreign occupations had two major effects. First, it broke the bond between law and legitimacy—formal institutions took on a theatrical aspect, while real power lay in those who could deliver outcomes. Second, it normalised unaccountable rule, judged not by legality but by effectiveness—who could protect, punish, and preserve order.

Mosca absorbed this logic from his native land. His essays depict sovereignty as negotiation, not doctrine—shaped by overlapping forces, shifting loyalties, and improvised control.[9] Sicily's history taught its people to rely on persons, not laws; to trust networks, not constitutions. The mafia did not disrupt this order—it extended it, adapting old patterns to a new national context.

Through Mosca's lens, we learn important political truths. Where the state lacks roots, power moves underground. Where rule arrives intermittently, informal authority settles in. Sicily's past, in his hands, became a case study in how sovereignty fragments—and how rule survives through other means.

Mosca's Lived Observation of Sicilian Society

Mosca's authority as an analyst of Sicilian society derives from his dual vantage point as both native and elite. As a Sicilian raised amid the codes of local life, and as a member of Italy's administrative class, Mosca possessed both intimacy and detachment. Born in Palermo and educated on the island before entering national institutions, Mosca carried with him the post-Risorgimento bourgeois perspective. But he also had firsthand knowledge of how power functioned informally—how honour, distrust, and patronage shaped daily life. He recognised how these patterns obstructed institutional development and trapped society in cycles of mutual suspicion.

This ambivalence gives his essays their distinctive tone. Mosca treated Sicily as a living case study, where one could

9 Gaetano Mosca. *The Ruling Class: A Study in Political Sociology.* Translated by Hannah D. Kahn (New York: McGraw-Hill, 1939), 14.

see clearly the materials of political power—social networks, symbolic authority, cultural memory, and coercion. His insider–outsider position also shaped his literary style. *Men and Things of Sicily* is rich in observation, anecdote, and character—not for colour, but because power is legible in gesture, not law. Crucially, his elite position allowed him to speak freely. He owed no allegiance to local patrons and had no need to flatter tradition. His essays at once condemn the mafia for its antisocial effect, while exposing the gap between legality and real control, showing how silence protects loyalty networks, and tracing how official forms mask entrenched monopolies.

Mosca treats the mafia above all as a "spirit" or mentality—not a single body but a diffuse complex of local cells whose members share a code of honour, an obligation to deceive the authorities (*omertà*), and a structure of small, independent clans (*cosche*) rather than a unified hierarchy. He characterises the mafia as less an "organisation" than a pervasive and antisocial mindset that thwarts the rule of law and entrenches informal power brokers across Sicilian society.

As a form of political ethnography, his writing places the reader amid real events—markets, elections, disputes—so that power can be observed in motion. He does not define it; he lets us see it negotiate, command, and conceal itself. His value lies in description, not theory. Each example sharpens the picture of a society ruled not by statute but by patterned behaviour.

IV. The Essays: Argument and Analysis

What Is the Mafia? – Key Insights in the 1900 Lecture

In *What Is the Mafia?*, Mosca treats the mafia not as a criminal aberration, but as an emergent social structure that functions in place of absent or weak state authority. For example, in section V:

> They take advantage of the submission and terror that an organized minority, capable of acting with calculation and unity, inspires in the disorganized majority, who dare not seek the protection of legal authorities.[10]

And in Section VIII:

> The protection once offered by nobles to petty criminals has now been replaced—and even surpassed—by the more effective protection provided by deputies, mayors, or councillors on behalf of influential mafia voters or prominent syndicate members.[11]

The mafioso is a man who cultivates the image of someone not to be wronged—resolving disputes, enforcing honour, and asserting power outside the courts. He does not stand apart from his society, but constitutes its operating system—embedded in kinship networks, prestige economies, and communal survival strategies.

Mosca's key insight is that the mafia functions as an alternative local authority, often filling roles that the official elite cannot or will not perform. The mafia supplements governance, rather than simply opposing it. While Mosca clearly prefers that law and justice flow through the state, we are left with the distinct impression that it need not do so—or more precisely, that whichever structure law and justice flows through constitutes the state. In practice, legitimacy follows whichever actor a community trusts to enforce order, and in Sicily, that often meant the mafia, not the judi-

10 p. 12.
11 pp. 23–24.

ciary. By analysing the mafia as a political institution, Mosca enables comparison with cartels, gangs, and informal power systems globally. In such contexts, the question is not who follows the law—but whose law holds sway.

By understanding sovereignty as the capacity to compel obedience—not merely the right to rule—we can see that where the state lacks this capacity, sovereignty reconstitutes itself elsewhere. In Sicily, the mafia built a parallel order grounded in fear, loyalty, and cultural legitimacy, which explains its durability. Its rule is not hidden, but semi-public—widely known yet officially denied.

> Although mafia leaders were widely known, the police could rely only on popular rumour rather than solid evidence. Few people dared to testify against the criminals in court, and even when a leader's responsibility for a crime was established, they often presented an alibi, while the "picciotti"—the foot soldiers who carried out the crimes—remained unknown.
>
> If the picciotti were arrested, they rarely provided any information about who had ordered them to commit the crime, as doing so would not only lead to their conviction but also strip them of their mafioso "honour" and sever their ties to the support traditionally provided by their cosca comrades who remained free.[12]

Mafia authority lacks codified law, yet its commands are followed. Mosca shows that it achieves a functional monopoly on coercion, fulfilling the sovereign role the state fails to occupy. Like Weber's later model of the state, this authority rests on force[13]—but force embedded in custom

12 "Mafia." *Encyclopaedia of the Social Sciences.*

13 Weber, Max. 1946. "Politics as a Vocation." In *From Max Weber: Essays in Sociology*, edited by H. H. Gerth and C. Wright Mills, 77–128. New York: Oxford University Press.

and expectation.

These essays are not simply critiques of criminality—they are studies of political order under failure. Mosca shows how governance persists where legality breaks down, and how authority consolidates without official sanction. His analysis remains prescient in a world increasingly shaped by informal power and fragmented legitimacy.

Men and Things of Sicily – Themes from the Essay Collection

Men and Things of Sicily shows Mosca at his most observational, resembling a form of political fieldwork. These essays do not offer abstract theory, but detailed portraits—of councillors, landowners, and municipal officials—that, taken together, reveal the inner architecture of Sicilian civic life. Rather than imposing a model, Mosca lets his subjects emerge through the accumulation of detail. Across the essays, what emerges is a portrait of governance in which institutional power is attenuated, and where individuals must navigate through unspoken codes of deference, expectation, and compromise.

In *Men and Things of Sicily*, Mosca shows how public authority often overlaps with private interest—what we would call "corruption". While he does not provide abstract theory, his essays imply a political culture shaped by familiarity, discretion, and the social management of office rather than impersonal legality. The most explicit example appears in his account of municipal councillors who, as practicing lawyers, represent private clients engaged in disputes with the same city governments they help administer.[14] This entanglement is not treated as scandalous—it is portrayed as

14 p. 71.

routine, a feature of how the system operates.

While Mosca does pass judgment on such arrangements, he is more concerned to document the mechanisms by which public roles are sustained through convention and mutual tolerance. These patterns, repeated across the essays, suggest a form of embedded order with its own expectations and codes. Mosca never calls this a system, but he makes clear that what liberal observers might view as dysfunction often appears locally as loyalty, prudence, or practical stewardship. His attention to such patterns anticipates later work on informal institutions and embedded authority—systems that endure precisely because they are legible and effective to those within them.[15]

Mosca's Sicily is not a land of chaos, but one of familiar rules—unwritten, enacted, and sustained through habit, relationship, and the slow choreography of civic life. At a time when political and journalistic voices framed the mafia as either a southern disgrace or a criminal pathology, Mosca broke with convention. He neither romanticised it nor condemned it with rhetorical outrage. Instead, he studied it as a form of authority that arises when formal governance collapses.

Mosca condemns the violence, extortion, and fear that mafiosi create, but he is aware that such condemnation still requires explanation. He describes the mafia as "a minority, capable of acting with calculation and unity," that dominates a disorganised majority left unprotected by public institutions. Because of this sober tone, *What Is the Mafia?* and the

15 See Gretchen Helmke and Steven Levitsky, "Informal Institutions and Comparative Politics: A Research Agenda," *Perspectives on Politics* 2, no. 4 (2004): 725–740. This article outlines how informal rules and norms can sustain political order and structure elite behaviour, particularly where formal institutions are weak or circumvented.

essays in *Men and Things of Sicily* received little attention as tools for reform. Yet their value has grown over time. Mosca's insistence on treating criminal authority as structurally embedded prefigures later work in political sociology and the study of hybrid regimes, where legality and coercion blur and state functions are informally outsourced.[16]

V. Relevance to the History of the Mafia and Organised Crime

Predictive Insight into 20th-Century Mafia Development

Although *What Is the Mafia?* predates the formal emergence of *la Cosa Nostra* ("our thing") as a centralised criminal organisation, Mosca's analysis anticipates its key structures. Lecturing in 1900, he captured the DNA of an institution that would evolve over the next century from loosely organised local networks into a transnational system of criminal governance. At the time, the mafia remained a diffuse phenomenon rooted in kinship, local patronage, and unwritten codes. Yet Mosca identified with remarkable precision the core elements that would later define *la Cosa Nostra*—coercive authority legitimated by honour and fear;[17] substitution for the state in dispensing justice and protection;[18] and internal cohesion based on loyalty, silence, and retribution.

As the mafia developed across the 20th century, especially during the interwar years and after WWII, it did not abandon its traditional roots—it formalised them. Rituals

16 See Thomas Bierschenk and Jean-Pierre Olivier de Sardan (eds.), *States at Work: Dynamics of African Bureaucracies* (Leiden: Brill, 2014), especially the introduction and chapters on informalisation and practical norms.

17 pp. 12–13.

18 p. 23.

like *omertà*, internal tribunals, and the codified rank system mirrored what Mosca had described decades earlier: an informal sovereignty based not on legality, but on functionality. Mosca grasped that this trajectory resembled not criminal evolution but state formation, with the mafia establishing territorial authority,[19] enforcing discipline,[20] collecting revenue,[21] and arbitrating disputes.[22]

Central to Mosca's foresight was his insistence that the mafia be seen as structural, not aberrant. Mafiosi did not stand outside society; they embodied its core values—honour, prestige, protection, and loyalty—and instrumentalised them. *La Cosa Nostra* succeeded by scaling these principles, extending its reach from rural Sicily to urban Italy, and even across the Atlantic. Even in its most modernised form, the mafia retained the tribal foundations Mosca had outlined—paternal leadership, symbolic authority, and the strategic use of violence.

By the late 20th century, magistrates like Falcone and Borsellino described a criminal regime that mirrored Mosca's vision—a parallel state, issuing orders, enforcing compliance, and shaping public life not just in southern Italy, but in the New World.[23] In mid-20th century American cities, Sicilian and southern Italian immigrants brought not only their labour and culture, but patterns of authority. These outsider communities recreated many of the conditions Mosca had documented in Sicily—distrust of the state, reliance on kinship and local mediation, and a preference

19 p. 15.

20 "Mafia." *Encyclopaedia of the Social Sciences.*

21 ibid.

22 p. 18.

23 Giovanni Falcone and Marcelle Padovani, *Cose di Cosa Nostra* (Milano: Rizzoli, 1991), esp. ch. 2–4.

for silence and honour over formal grievance. And just as in Mosca's Sicily, the mafia in America substituted for absent or distrusted institutions. It enforced contracts, offered credit, settled disputes, and protected its clients—demanding loyalty and silence in return.[24] Legitimacy came not from legality, but from effectiveness and cultural familiarity. Mafia figures often held more sway than elected officials, not out of affection, but because they delivered.

The American mafia's hierarchical structure—bosses, underbosses, capos, soldiers—mirrored Mosca's insight into informal governance. Its codes of conduct, internal courts, and initiation rites did not represent innovation, but the extension of an older political logic. *La Cosa Nostra* captured precisely what Mosca had described: a self-contained moral world bound by shared expectations of secrecy, honour, and enforcement. What Mosca implicitly foresaw, even if not in detail, was the mafia's ability to interface with modern capitalism and state institutions. Through unions, construction contracts, and municipal machines, mafia influence blurred the line between public power and private coercion. This was Mosca's Sicily on a larger scale—an informal regime operating in the twilight between illegality and legitimacy.

'Ndrangheta: The Amplification of Mosca's Model

While *What Is the Mafia?* focuses on early 20th-century Sicily, the conceptual tools Mosca develops apply with even greater force to the *'Ndrangheta* of Calabria. Though less publicly mythologised, the *'Ndrangheta* has become Italy's most powerful and globalised mafia organisation.

Where *la Cosa Nostra* eventually adopted a semi-centralised structure, the *'Ndrangheta* remained atomised and

24 Diego Gambetta, *The Sicilian Mafia: The Business of Private Protection* (Cambridge, MA: Harvard University Press, 1993), 17–24.

intensely familial. Its core unit, the *'ndrina*, is a blood-bound clan. Membership is hereditary. Loyalty is not a bureaucratic ideal—it is a kin obligation. Betrayal constitutes not just institutional failure, but familial desecration. In this sense, the *'Ndrangheta* more fully embodies the tribal structures Mosca described in embryonic form: rule not by abstract authority, but by ancestral bond.

Calabria, like Sicily, has long endured marginalisation and fragmented state presence. In this vacuum, the *'Ndrangheta* emerged in place of the state, governing through custom, vengeance, protection, and kinship honour. It does not publicly mediate power as the Sicilian mafia sometimes did, but rather internalises it. *Omertà* in this context is instinctive, enforced by blood and reinforced through ritual. Authority, discipline, and mediation operate not through impersonal networks but through flesh and blood. This grants it a degree of cohesion and opacity that exceeds even *la Cosa Nostra*.

What makes the *'Ndrangheta* exceptional in the modern era is that it scaled without compromising its structure. From the 1970s onward, it expanded into northern Italy, Germany, Switzerland, Canada, and Australia—embedding itself in diaspora communities and financial systems. Unlike the American mafia, which gradually shed its traditionalism, the *'Ndrangheta* exported its model intact. Each transplanted *'ndrina* retained the same rules, rites, and blood-bonds, functioning as autonomous cells bound by ancestral allegiance.

This evolution reinforces Mosca's insight—when informal power is deeply embedded, it becomes adaptive, culturally persistent, and capable of regenerating itself in new settings.[25] The *'Ndrangheta's* pre-modern, decentralised, kin-based form allows it to adapt flexibly to diverse legal regimes without fracturing. It marries tribal loyalty to global logistical sophistication, exerting control in arenas from narcotics to construction, from rural Calabria to European ports. Had Mosca witnessed this development, he likely would have seen the *'Ndrangheta* as the perfected embodiment of his theory: a social organism whose sovereignty is enforced not through legal code but through ritual, honour, and kinship—extended now across a transnational stage. Its longevity affirms Mosca's insight: that rule rooted in cultural embeddedness, affective bonds, and informal legitimacy often outlasts the formal institutions that seek to suppress it.[26]

In this way, the *'Ndrangheta* represents an amplification of Mosca's model. His analysis captures not only resistance to the state, but its quiet replacement by more intimate, adaptable, and enduring forms of rule. The deeper the social roots, Mosca shows, the more resilient the regime—no matter how "modern" the world around it becomes.

Camorra, Japanese Yakuza, Russian Bratva, and Latin American Cartels

While *What Is the Mafia?* focuses narrowly on turn-of-the-century Sicily, Mosca's framework has broad global application. The *Camorra*, *Yakuza*, *Bratva*, and Latin American cartels each operate in different settings, but they all confirm Mosca's core insight. These are not criminal anomalies—they are political responses to institutional failure.

The *Camorra*, rooted in Naples, contrasts with *la Cosa Nostra's* hierarchy. It is decentralised, factional, and oppor-

25 p. 7.
26 p. 23.

tunistic—less a single organisation than a fluid network of competing clans. Yet it thrives, not despite its fragmentation, but because of its deep entanglement in the urban informal economy. It distributes loans, enforces contracts, and manages street-level order in places where the state is ineffective.[27]

The *Yakuza* in Japan reflects a more overt form of informal sovereignty. Its members historically registered with the state, operated out of open offices, and mediated disputes in plain sight. Despite being extra-legal, the *Yakuza* long functioned as a visible auxiliary to state order, particularly in times of crisis.[28] The central insight of these texts—that legitimacy flows from efficacy, not legality[29]—is here made explicit.

In Russia, the *Bratva* took Mosca's framework further still. Following the Soviet collapse, organised crime merged with state power itself. The *Bratva* infiltrated political office, national industries, and security services—transforming from informal authority into ruling class.[30] This is Mosca's ruling class theory realised in its starkest form: criminal elites rising not outside the state, but through it, stabilising their dominance via access to coercion, capital, and institutional continuity.

Latin American cartels, particularly in Mexico and Colombia, offer yet another example of Mosca's insight. These groups do not merely smuggle, they regulate trade, dispense

27 Felia Allum, *Camorristi, Politicians and Businessmen: The Transformation of Organized Crime in Post-War Naples*, vol. 11 (London: Routledge, 2006), 286.

28 Peter B. E. Hill, *The Japanese Mafia: Yakuza, Law, and the State* (Oxford: Oxford University Press, 2003), 45–47.

29 p. 23.

30 Mark Galeotti, *The Vory: Russia's Super Mafia* (London: Yale University Press, 2018), 45–47.

justice, maintain order, and at times enjoy greater legitimacy than state forces.[31] Like the mafia, their rule is enforced through fear, but legitimised by predictability and provision of *de facto* law in abandoned regions. They are structurally functional authorities filling a sovereign void.

What unites all these cases is not cultural similarity, but political ecology. Where the state cannot enforce norms or command trust, parallel structures arise. These entities succeed not because they are criminal *per se*, but because they organise coercion, distribute resources, and offer stability in ways the formal system cannot.

While Mosca certainly moralises at times and takes a consistently condemnatory tone, his contribution lies in going beyond moral framing to expose how power actually works. Whether in Naples or Michoacán, Osaka or Moscow, his insight holds—sovereignty is not defined by legality, but by who can rule, enforce, and be recognised as doing so.

VI. Contemporary Relevance: Tribalisation and the Return of Local Sovereignties

Resurgence of Non-State Authority in the 21st Century

In the 21st century, Mosca's central insight has moved from Sicilian parochialism to global condition. Across cities and regions in both the West and the Global South, we now see informal regimes filling the void left by the retreat of national legitimacy. In modern urban centres—London,

31 International Institute for Strategic Studies, "The Expansion and Diversification of Mexican Cartels: Dynamic New Actors and Markets," *Armed Conflict Survey 2024*, https://www.iiss.org/publications/armed-conflict-survey/2024/the-expansion-and-diversification-of-mexican-cartels-dynamic-new-actors-and-markets.

Paris, Chicago, Stockholm—the rise of enclaves is replacing national integration. Even outside impoverished areas, legitimacy is fracturing. Among the wealthy, distrust in law enforcement and national institutions has produced gated communities with private security. The mechanism is the same: when trust in shared institutions dies, people turn inward—to kin, identity, belief, and proximity.

Political polarisation in the West has eroded even symbolic consensus.[32] Courts, elections, and parliaments are no longer universally recognised; each group recognises only what mirrors its worldview. Rule is returning to the local and the familiar.[33] The central question is no longer whether we have order, but who controls it, and under what terms.

The 21st century has seen the global spread of non-state actors exercising real, coercive authority—often more effective, more feared, and more entrenched than the governments they displace.[34] In Western cities, ethnic gangs have filled the vacuum left by weak integration and distrust in national institutions. Somali, Albanian, Kurdish, and South Sudanese groups in Europe; African-American, Latino, and Asian gangs in the U.S.; Pashtun and Chechen networks in Eurasia—all function as authority structures within ethnic enclaves. In failed or fragile states, cartels and warlords have

32 For more on this, see Imperium Press, *The Epistemic Divorce*. https://imperiumpress.substack.com/p/the-epistemic-divorce.

33 Alexander Bastianen and Nicolas Keuffer, "Exploring the Impact of Local Autonomy on Democratic Legitimacy," *Decentralization Net*, July 30, 2024, https://decentralization.net/2024/07/exploring-the-impact-of-local-autonomy-on-democratic-legitimacy/.

34 Michael von der Schulenburg, "The Era of Armed Non-State Actors: Risks of Global Chaos," *Changing Character of Conflict Platform*, University of Oxford, February 14, 2020, https://www.globalsecurity.pmb.ox.ac.uk/research-and-publications/research/michael-von-der-schulenburg-the-era-of-armed-non-state-actors-risks-of-global-chaos.

advanced even further, assuming open governance roles. In Mexico and Colombia, cartels build roads, distribute aid, and hold public ceremonies.[35] In Somalia, Congo, Helmand, and northern Syria, militias regulate trade, issue fines, and settle disputes.[36] These are not outlaw groups; they are alternative states all but in but name.

Many of these actors now operate transnationally. Cartels cross borders with impunity. Ethnic gangs form diaspora networks. Warlords secure funds through extractive industries and global markets. They are not relics of the past—they are products of the present, because the age of trans-continental nations of millions is passing. Today, what counts as "the nation" is devolving before our very eyes.

These groups reflect the same structural features Mosca identified: extra-legal but embedded; feared yet respected; decentralised but stable. His insights from the first decades of the 20th century help us to see the new sovereigns of the 21st century clearly—rulers without states, commanding loyalty in spaces where law no longer rules.

Mosca's Relevance to Today's Multicultural Urban Politics

In recent decades, liberal democratic cities—especially in Western Europe, North America, and Oceania—have

35 Videos of Drug Cartels Handing Out Aid Challenge Mexican Authorities," *The Wall Street Journal*, April 23, 2020, https://www.wsj.com/video/series/news-explainers/videos-of-drug-cartels-handing-out-aid-challenge-mexican-authorities/6C25E3E7-7F5F-4F8B-877E-159FA01A8646.

36 Vanda Felbab-Brown, "The Problem with Militias in Somalia: Almost Everyone Wants Them, Despite Their Dangers," *Brookings Institution*, September 12, 2018, https://www.brookings.edu/articles/the-problem-with-militias-in-somalia-almost-everyone-wants-them-despite-their-dangers/.

undergone a shift in governance and composition. Once defined by dominant cultural norms, urban centres have become mosaics of ethnic, linguistic, and religious enclaves with parallel customs and informal institutions. While multiculturalism promised coexistence under a shared liberal framework, the reality is that certain communities now function as *de facto* autonomous zones, governed less by state law than by honour codes, religious rulings, and communal enforcement.

This exposes a central tension in the liberal order—passive toleration risks parallel sovereignties; active intervention risks violating multicultural principles. In practice, the state often defaults to passive toleration, mirroring the deference Mosca documented in Italy, where local power was accommodated rather than confronted.[37] This is not just a failure of integration—it is a sovereignty crisis. In this world, the liberal state may persist in form, but it often competes with embedded micro-sovereignties it cannot displace, or cannot afford to displace.

Examples abound: in areas of London, Berlin, Brussels, Malmö, Rotterdam, and Paris, sharia councils, clan elders, and community tribunals handle issues of marriage, debt, and behaviour, often outside the national legal system.[38] Participation may appear voluntary, but costs for dissent—ostracism, reputational harm, or violent retaliation—render them effectively compulsory. The state, meanwhile, often tolerates them, whether to ease administrative burdens or avoid cultural backlash.

37 pp. 23, 165, 108.

38 David James Smith, "Sharia London: Surge in Back-Room Councils That Rule on Muslim Marriages," *The Standard*, April 21, 2025, https://www.standard.co.uk/news/islamic-sharia-council-law-london-marriage-divorce-b1222943.html.

David Betz's Thesis: The West Enters Dirty Civil War

David Betz's concept of a "dirty civil war"—a diffuse, informal conflict consisting of low-level violence beyond the purview of the state—closely parallels Mosca's early diagnosis of internal sovereignty collapse. While Betz describes the disintegration of institutional authority in the contemporary West, Mosca mapped the same structural logic in early 20th-century Sicily—the erosion of belief in central institutions, the rise of alternative sources of legitimacy, and the fragmentation of civic loyalty.

> It is not simply that the conditions [for civil war] are present in the West; it is, rather, that the conditions are nearing the ideal. The relative wealth, social stability and related lack of demographic factionalism, plus the perception of the ability of normal politics to solve problems that once made the West seem immune to civil war are now no longer valid. In fact, in each of these categories the direction of pull is *towards* civil conflict.[39]

Mosca did not speak of civil war, but he showed how the liberal state's formal presence in Sicily masked its practical irrelevance. Governance had shifted to a parallel structure—the mafia—which resolved disputes, imposed order, and commanded obedience. In Betz's terms, Mosca had already described a "dirty" war. Today, Betz sees something similar in Britain and America. Institutions persist, but their authority is filtered through ideological, and increasingly ethnic loyalties. Laws are passed, elections are held, but their legitimacy is no longer assumed. Policing in ethnic enclaves

39 David Betz, "Civil War Comes to the West," *Military Strategy Magazine* 9, no. 1 (Summer 2023): 20–26, https://www.militarystrategymagazine.com/article/civil-war-comes-to-the-west/.

is "negotiated"—courts are respected or ignored depending on the needs of the community.

As with Mosca, we find implied in David Betz's "dirty civil war" thesis that the erosion of formal sovereignty does not produce chaos, but the emergence of informal regimes of rule operating beneath the threshold of state control. Just as the mafia settled disputes in areas where state law was distrusted or absent, contemporary communities—particularly in ethnic enclaves—increasingly turn to gang leaders, religious figures, or local councils to resolve conflict, whose justice is backed by coercive power, not abstract legitimacy. In today's West, that power may come from gangs, militias, or community-aligned security groups. These actors do not openly oppose the state, but they do not need to—they enforce order where it no longer functions.

Betz's dirty civil war thus reflects a layered system of governance in which the state competes with rivals whose justice is immediate, whose violence is credible, and whose loyalty is enforced. The West is not collapsing into disorder, but stratifying into contested sovereignties, and herein lies Mosca's lasting relevance.

Mosca as an Early Theorist of Fragmentation

One of the most enduring and misunderstood aspects of Mosca's political theory is his claim that all societies are governed by elites—not normatively, but as a structural fact. The central variable is not whether elites rule, but which elites do, and how. Mosca thus becomes a theorist not only of elite continuity, but of political fragmentation. He saw that while elite rule is constant, its form mutates as institutions dissolve and power devolves across informal axes. Classical liberalism assumed that modernisation would yield rational, transparent elites—civil servants, legislators, experts. But Mosca, writing from Sicily's political margins, understood that formal institutions do not eliminate older structures. Where state reach or trust is weak, embedded elites replace it. In this shift, Mosca's insight proves prescient: elites do not need office to rule—only a "political formula" that legitimises their authority, however local, tribal, or affective it may be. Modern politics is thus not de-elitised, but retribalised.

In the 21st century, governance will depend on mapping these plural elites. Elite bodies have always exhibited some degree of factional division. But as sovereignty devolves, we may no longer find ourselves governed by a singular "ruling class," but clusters of functional rulers—operating through codes, patronage, and presence rather than legal bureaucracy. In this world, liberal tools—law, procedure, equality—will count for less than honour, coercion, and embeddedness. Elite rule will not vanish; it will adapt. Mosca understood that politics does not end when institutions collapse, it changes.

VII. Conclusion

Mosca's Dual Value

Gaetano Mosca's *What Is the Mafia?* is more than a historical study of Sicily—it is a diagnostic framework for understanding how political order functions when the state is present in name but absent in effect. Drawing on his unique position as both a Sicilian native and a national political theorist, Mosca offered a rare, clear-eyed account of para-sovereignty in action: a world where power operates through honour, coercion, and reciprocity, not through law or central authority. In this light, Mosca's work anticipates contemporary challenges. Turn-of-the-century Sicily is no longer exceptional—it is a prototype for the post-nationalist world emerging today.

If Mosca's first value lies in his sharp-eyed account of

Sicily's para-sovereign order, his greater value lies in his role as an architect of political realism—a thinker who grasped how power endures when formal authority falters. Mosca understood, long before Schmitt or Huntington, that law follows power, not the reverse. Mosca considered himself a liberal, and his ruling class thesis was not an attack on liberalism *per se* but a structural account of how politics actually works. Every society, he argued, is ruled by an organised minority. Elections may rotate elites, but they do not abolish them. The machinery of government—whether liberal or autocratic—runs on organisation, loyalty, and strategic enforcement, not on idealist abstractions.

This placed Mosca in tension with democratic optimism. While democrats assumed that participation and reform could perfect governance, Mosca saw elite dominance as inevitable. When central institutions lose cultural traction, rule does not vanish—it reverts to embedded networks: kinship, faction, patronage. That reversion is now increasingly visible. In fractured democracies and post-liberal regimes, informal sovereignties flourish—within ethnic enclaves, new elites have begun to operate beneath the shell of statehood. Mosca gave us a vocabulary to name this: rule without office, justice without courts, legitimacy without legality, power beyond law.

Enduring Importance of the Works in This Volume

At first glance, the writings in this volume—*What Is the Mafia?* and *Men and Things of Sicily*—may appear to belong to a vanished world. They describe life in a remote region of Italy over a century ago, filled with agricultural disputes, ritual violence, and coded silences. But to treat them as quaint relics would be to misread them entirely. These are not nostalgic accounts of rustic criminality, but case studies in political order under conditions of state weakness—blueprints for understanding how power reconfigures itself when central authority falters. Mosca teaches us that when states recede, legitimacy does not collapse—it reconstitutes itself in smaller, more intimate forms. Justice and order will always be sought, and when the state cannot deliver them, others will.

As liberal institutions erode, as state sovereignty becomes contested, and as loyalty shifts from abstract nationhood to local identity, we are re-entering the world Mosca described—a world of plural sovereignties, informal justice, and pragmatic enforcement. These texts must be read not only as reports from the past, but as guides to an emerging future, where governance is not monopolised by the state, but exercised by those who can act, protect, and compel.

EDWARD MAXWELL III
May 2024

Bibliographic References

Journal Articles and Magazine Essays

"Cosa è la Mafia." *Giornale degli Economisti*, July 1901, 236–62.

"The Municipalization of Bread in Palermo in the XVII and XVIII Centuries." *La Lettura* (Supplement of *Corriere della Sera*), 1902.

Newspaper Articles

"The Palermo Inquiry." *Corriere della Sera*, January 18–19, 1902.

"Palermo and the Pro-Palizzolo Agitation." *Corriere della Sera*, August 18, 1902.

"Why the Apotheosis of Palizzolo Offends Morality." *Corriere della Sera*, July 29, 1904.

"The Galantuomini." *Corriere della Sera*, September 1, 1905.

"Parties." *Corriere della Sera*, October 4, 1905.

"Latifundia and Peasant Farmers." *Corriere della Sera*, September 27, 1905.

"Why Hasn't the Belief in State-Sponsored Poisoning Disappeared?" *Corriere della Sera*, September 17, 1911.

"The Nasi Phenomenon Judged by a Sicilian." *Corriere della Sera*, September 27, 1908.

"The Death of Antonio Rudinì." *Corriere della Sera*, August 8, 1908.

Books and Edited Volumes

Uomini e cose di Sicilia. Palermo: Sellerio editore, 1980.

What Is the Mafia?

I.

Regarding the recent and now famous trial in Milan, much has been said and written about the mafia—an age-old issue that periodically gains new interest and relevance.[1]

It is rather strange that those who discuss and write about the mafia throughout Italy, especially in the north, still rarely have a precise and exact understanding of what the word "mafia" encompasses. Truth be told, it should have been the Sicilians themselves who clarified the missing aspects and established the true meaning of this term they introduced into the national dictionary. However, to the Sicilians, their region's complex social phenomena and anomalies, which they succinctly describe as *la mafia*, have become so familiar that they almost don't realize others might need a detailed explanation or precise definition to understand the various meanings of the term that the island's natives easily distinguish through their long-standing customs.

1 The trial mentioned, which took place in 1899 and will be revisited by Mosca, refers to the first investigation into the murder of Emanuele Notarbartolo by a mafia clan. Notarbartolo was an eminent nobleman from Palermo, a renowned Sicilian politician, and a former director of the Bank of Sicily.

Since the first step is to eliminate this vagueness in our spoken language, we must recognize that Sicilians use the word "mafia" to refer to two distinct occurrences or social phenomena. Although these phenomena are strongly related, they can be analysed separately. The mafia, or rather the spirit of mafia, is a mindset that—similar to haughtiness, pride, and overbearingness—within a certain social order, necessitates adopting a particular line of conduct. In Sicily, the term does not refer to a specific fellowship but to a vast complex of many small associations, each with its own goals and aspirations. These goals and aspirations are such that they invariably bring the members of these associations perilously close to violating the penal code and can sometimes involve truly criminal behaviour.

II.

The feeling, or rather the spirit of mafia, can be described in a few words: it involves viewing the use of official justice, the police, and the judiciary to address wrongs—as well as certain received wrongs—as a sign of weakness or cowardice. While it is generally accepted, even by those who operate according to the norms of the mafia spirit, that simple theft, fraud, freeloading, and other crimes relying solely on cunning and deceit without the use of violence or displaying greater strength and courage than the victim can be reported to the authorities, this is prohibited when the crime becomes an open and shameless imposition. In such cases, the perpetrator specifically intends to harm a particular individual to assert their own superiority. They do not fear enmity or resentment and have no interest in maintaining good relations, which a false sense of honour or personal dignity prevents them from reporting these more personal and aggressive crimes to the authorities.

Offenses against a family's honour, beatings, personal

violence, and murder committed in a brawl or by ambush are all crimes that the mafia considers inappropriate and cowardly to report, viewing such reporting as a form of chivalric disqualification. However, these are not the only offenses treated this way. Acts like cutting vines, killing livestock, cattle rustling, and even robbery and extortion with kidnapping—when they take on the character of personal revenge or an insult directed at a specific individual—are also technically not reportable. If these crimes are reported, it is merely a formality to comply with the law [*per mettersi in regola*], as they say in Sicily, without actually aiding in the discovery of the perpetrator, who is often well known and intended to feel the weight of personal revenge.

It is worth noting that the characteristic of revenge and offense directed at a specific person is a true hallmark of Sicilian criminality. In Sicily, crimes that elsewhere would have no personal motive and are typically committed by professional criminals who choose their victims indiscriminately from those available, instead appear as acts of revenge for a real or supposed wrong that the perpetrator, or some of their relatives or friends, may have suffered at the hands of the victim. It should be understood that often the mentioned wrong is not the true cause but rather a pretext for the criminal act.

It is for this reason that Italians from the mainland and, in general, all foreigners who travel to or live in Sicily are almost always respected by wrongdoers. This is because foreigners typically do not have dealings with the criminal class, making them difficult targets for personal vendettas. It is also for this same reason that Sicilians living in the island's large cities are rarely victims of premeditated crimes. In large cities, everyone can freely choose the people with whom they want to establish relationships, and personal grievances are less likely to flare up and do not find nourishment in daily contacts and friction as they do in smaller towns.

It is important to note that the principle established for preventing and addressing a broad category of personal offenses is that a man who wants and knows how to command respect [*sa farsi rispettare*]—using the technical term—should not resort to legal justice. Consequently, it is permissible, and indeed obligatory, to deceive the authorities or at least withhold information when they attempt to interfere in private disputes by disrupting their natural course with criminal code rules. Therefore, a direct result of the mafia mentality is the code of silence [*l'omertà*], the rule that it is dishonourable to provide information to the authorities about crimes that the mafia believes should be resolved between the offending and offended parties. This rule, which also applies to disputes between third parties, is the main reason why witnesses in criminal trials often become deceitful or, rather, evasive. For Sicilians, even those from the poorest and roughest classes, outright lying is rare. Instead of telling falsehoods, they frequently claim that they do not know or do not remember the truth, which they actually know and remember very well.

I have met educated people from northern Italy who find something proud and appealing, or at least not entirely ignoble, in this mafia sentiment or spirit—where each individual believes it is honourable to rely on their own strength and courage to repel and prevent offenses. However, sometimes a way of thinking and feeling, even with not entirely ignoble motives, can produce overall harmful results. In such cases, we must have the courage to condemn it vigorously and without excuses. The mafia spirit is essentially an antisocial sentiment that prevents true order and genuine justice from being established and becoming effective among populations deeply affected by it. As we will see later, it also ultimately results in the oppression of the weak by the strong and the tyranny exercised by small organized minorities at the expense of individuals in the disorganized majority.

One could more reasonably observe that the mafia spirit is not unique to Sicily; it has been found and is still found in many other parts of the world where social justice has emerged or has proven incapable of completely uprooting and replacing the system of private vengeance. Indeed, the mafia spirit, though much diminished, still exists in central Italy and, in an even more attenuated form, in northern Italy. While the term originated in Sicily, this is because, due to circumstances that may need to be explored in the history of the recent or fading century, *mafiosità* is more deeply rooted, more widespread, and more profound there. It has also become more disciplined and organized in Sicily. Similarly, the Jesuits gave their name to Jesuitism, which they did not invent nor are they its only devotees, but they have practiced and still practice it assiduously, refining and systematizing it through their constant dedication.

In many parts of central Italy, the common people still believe that the police officer, the cop [lo sbirro], is a vile being and disapprove of anyone who reveals the assailant's name to justice when injured in a brawl. Thus, not only does the mafia exist there, but it also has its inseparable companion, the code of silence. While workers in Turin are generally immune to this plague, in the very lowest strata of the city—among the destitute and petty criminals—a perfectly analogous way of operating is still in force and honoured.

But even among the upper classes of much of Europe and all of Italy, a slight spirit of the mafia still exists. It is acknowledged that for certain personal offenses, reparation should not be sought through legal justice but through a duel. After all, the duel is merely a form—attenuated, regulated, and surrounded by guarantees—of the bloody contests between two individuals that the common people of Sicily and all of southern and central Italy often use to resolve their disputes.

III.

It is difficult to precisely determine how widespread the mafia spirit is in Sicily. First, one must establish where the mafia mentality begins and ends. Certainly, if one rigorously examines each Sicilian individually, labelling as mafiosi anyone who, in a particular situation, prefers to handle an arrogant person or offender with their own hands rather than resorting to justice, it could be claimed that the mafia includes the majority of the island's inhabitants. However, if we apply broader and more just criteria—considering someone a mafioso only if they have committed a crime out of a mafia spirit or are at least capable of doing so—then the number of Sicilians who, as the Northern Italians say, are affiliated with the mafia becomes a small minority.

If we distinguish based on the various social classes and regions of the island, I would say that the mafia spirit is generally stronger and more widespread in small towns than in large cities, where it is significantly less present. Furthermore, the poorest peasants in the interior of the island are less affected by it than the more affluent and educated ones in the towns near Palermo and the surrounding rural villages. It is also natural that the mafia spirit is generally stronger among the poor and unrefined classes rather than among the wealthy and, above all, the educated, despite what might be said or written to the contrary. However, it must be acknowledged that a significant portion of the poorer classes, consisting of those who practice certain specific trades, is almost completely immune to it; this is particularly true for sailors and fishermen, who are very numerous on the island. It is also true that some segments of the ruling classes, including certain wealthy and even noble families, are deeply infused with mafia tendencies. However, these often include families of *gabellotti* (land leaseholders) or large tenants of rural estates who have recently become wealthy, where education and culture have lagged behind wealth by one or two generations. Alternatively, if they are ancient noble families, they often possess a good dose of ignorance and rusticity along with their noble titles, poorly disguised by a peculiar gentility. Living mostly in isolated villages, where modern ideas and sentiments have had little influence, they have, if I may use the metaphor, taken on the moral character of their surrounding environment.

Within the same family, or even within the same individual, the mafia spirit can increase, decrease, or disappear depending on whether the person moves to a different environment. A Sicilian who goes to the mainland, to places where mafia behaviour is considered low and vulgar, quickly sheds any trace of the mafia spirit thanks to the remarkable intuition and extraordinary adaptability that distinguish him. The same happens, to a lesser degree, with a Sicilian who moves from a small mafia-influenced town to Palermo, Messina, or Catania. Conversely, in certain small rural communities where turning to the regular justice system is seen as ineffective—perhaps because it is rarely used and does not help the individual gain respect—even a Sicilian from the big cities who stays there for a long time acquires a strong mafia influence. This influence can even affect people from northern Italy who settle in these areas.

However, I have witnessed that natives of towns and rural villages deeply and traditionally steeped in the mafia spirit, if they live long enough in the large cities of the island or on the Italian mainland and acquire a solid and broad intellectual culture, undergo a true psychological transformation. As a result of this transformation, they develop an invincible aversion to permanently returning to their ancestral home. Due to this psychological change, they gain such respect for the rule of law and such disgust for private violence that, in this regard, they are by no means inferior to the most honourable gentlemen of northern Italy. This alone, even if other arguments are lacking, would be enough to prove that the mafia is not the result of inheritance or race, but of the environment in which one lives.

It often happens that an Italian from Northern Italy will confidentially ask a Sicilian friend whether a certain fellow Sicilian is a mafioso and receive an affirmative answer. While the response is usually given in good faith, it should always be taken with a grain of salt. To obtain truly conclusive information, at least a few more precise questions are needed. For a Sicilian, anyone who is slightly more mafioso than himself is considered a mafioso—meaning someone who, even theoretically, supports a somewhat broader use of private action and force to prevent or repel potential offenses. Therefore, the label "mafioso" can easily be applied to someone who is not affiliated with any criminal organization, has never committed a crime, and might perhaps be incapable of committing one.

The immortal Manzoni, the greatest sociologist of modern Italy and renowned for his deep psychological insights, describes Renzo (the male protagonist of "The Betrothed," Manzoni's magnum opus and perhaps Italy's greatest novel) as having "a certain air of common bravado [*braveria*], which was also evident among the quietest men of that time." While it would be a true exaggeration to compare today's Sicily to Lombardy during the time of "The Betrothed" (the 17th century), traces of that era can still be found more vividly and enduringly on the island of Sicily than in Northern Italy. Therefore, a certain air of bravado—or, if you prefer, a certain scent of mafia—is still much more widespread in Sicily, even among honest men, than in Piedmont, Veneto, or Lombardy.

Above all, and this is the region's true specialty, while in Northern Italy the aforementioned scent can be perceived only in the very lowest social strata, in Sicily it can still be found—though sporadically—but nevertheless quite intensely, even among individuals of the higher classes. These individuals sometimes hold prominent positions that confer significant authority and suggest that they enjoy the esteem of their fellow citizens.

IV.

Perhaps the greatest damage caused by the spread of the mafia mentality, across all social classes but especially in the higher ones, lies in the fact that it is very difficult to be influenced by it and to follow its precepts without, to some extent, entering into relationships and connections with the lowest strata of society, from which professional criminals are recruited. Thrust among these socially disenfranchised groups, where custom dictates the use of private rather than public force to prevent and suppress wrongs, offenses, and crimes, it is easy to understand the many troubles that an isolated individual must endure—especially one who does not know or is unable to rebel against this custom and who is not protected by numerous friendships and connections among those most capable of committing wrongs, offenses, and crimes.

Therefore, in those parts of Sicily where mafia-like behaviour is most prevalent, a wealthy and prominent man of high standing who wishes to take an active part in local life and become, as they say, a public figure is easily led to cultivate various relationships. These relationships are ultimately maintained through a series of protections and favours. In return, the distinguished individual receives the respect of those below him. This respect is shown not only through bows and deference but also, and more importantly, by refraining from causing any harm or offense to the respected person, their family, their property, and even their friends. Additionally, it involves preventing others from doing so and offering unconditional support for their aspirations to elective positions.

The mafia spirit also ensures that some high-ranking individuals—mayors, councillors, provincial representatives, and sometimes even deputies—either do not feel, or feel only a very diminished sense of repulsion towards troublemakers or individuals capable of committing crimes, which a truly honourable person would experience. Thus, the high-ranking mafioso is easily inclined to intercede with the authorities on behalf of his low-status friend, and he does not abandon him to his fate unless the latter has committed so many and such serious offenses that it becomes truly impossible to prevent him from ending up in the nation's prisons.

The friendship between the wealthy, influenced by the mafia spirit, and poor troublemakers naturally includes endless variations, depending on circumstances and the different personalities of the individuals involved. Some wealthy individuals maintain a certain reserve in their dealings with low-level criminals, never allowing true criminals into their service or close circles, and only using their connections with the lower mafia for defensive purposes. Others take a perverse pleasure in associating with shady characters, surrounding themselves with murderers and ex-convicts, and even going so far as to incite them to harm the property and persons of their enemies. Among the poor mafiosi, there are those who have committed or are always ready to commit actual crimes, as well as those who limit themselves to appearing as resolute men—people with guts who, when necessary, could respond with violence. They display just enough mafioso behaviour to be considered important and to maintain mutually respectful relationships with the wealthy, which are so useful to the poor.

It must be stated that, even in the most morally corrupt parts of Sicily, there are both poor and wealthy individuals who, without openly and systematically rebelling against the land's customs, reluctantly tolerate and endure them. They never commit acts of oppression, much less crimes, nor do they present themselves as capable of such acts. These individuals, if poor, easily become victims of harassment from their peers and the whims of their masters; if wealthy, they must renounce many legitimate ambitions, and their assets are often targeted by criminals.

I am assured, however, that although this may harm their finances, the monetary damage they suffer is almost always less than what they would incur from having overly close and friendly relationships with the criminals themselves.

This means that the wealthy and high-ranking individuals who cultivate such relationships do not do so out of unavoidable necessity, as they often claim to authorities and to their friends and acquaintances in Palermo and other cities on the island less steeped in mafioso culture. Rather, they do it out of ambition, vanity, and a desire to excel in the mafia-dominated environments to which they have perfectly adapted.

V.

However, the most harmful consequence of the mafia spirit is that it allows a large number of small criminal associations to gain extraordinary vitality. Together, these form another Sicilian peculiarity I mentioned at the beginning of the lecture, which Sicilians collectively refer to with the broad and all-encompassing term "mafia."

However, in the rich dialect of the island, there is a specific expression to designate these associations. Each is called a "*cosca di mafia*," or simply a "*cosca*" ['*koska*']. When someone is said to be "*della cosca*" (of the clan), it means they are part of one of these dishonourable groups.

Allow me to point out that a faint version of the Sicilian phenomenon can also be found in other regions of Italy. The word "cosca," used to indicate an association of people involved in a life of crime, with a slight variation, is not unknown in northern Italy. In Turin, for instance, there have been times when the *barabba* (street thugs) organized into groups or societies called "*coche*," such as the Coca di Porta Palazzo and the Coca di Vanchiglia, just as, unfortunately, in Sicily there are still the Cosca di Altavilla and the Cosca di Villabate. However, the mafioso cosca in Sicily has much stronger cohesion, greater force of action, and, above all, an infinitely superior vitality compared to the Coca Barabesca in Turin.

This greater vitality, along with the continuous emergence and re-emergence of the cosche, is primarily due, as I have already briefly mentioned, to the spirit of the mafia. The mafia serves as the true breeding ground where all harmful elements and criminal associations can live and thrive. Indeed, when there is a widespread belief that reporting perpetrators of certain crimes to justice is an ineffective sign of weakness, it becomes natural for professional criminals—the scum of the social underworld—to band together. They take advantage of the submission and terror that an organized minority, capable of acting with calculation and unity, inspires in the disorganized majority, who dare not seek the protection of legal authorities.

To fully understand the effectiveness of the mafia sentiment, it is important to recognize that it is not only fear in the strict sense—the fear of material harm—that makes victims and witnesses hesitant to accuse members of a cosca openly when they commit a crime. Alongside this fear is *omertà* (the code of silence), an aversion to appearing weaker than the offender by resorting to justice to seek redress for harm. This aversion, even if it manifests as a form of moral fear, serves to mask and justify material fear in the eyes of the individual and their associates. Moreover, physical fear is sometimes cited as an excuse for moral fear when addressing people from Northern Italy, for whom the mafia spirit seems both incomprehensible and entirely unjustifiable.

That's not all: another psychological factor contributes to the reluctance of many witnesses, one that stems from a less base origin but is no less effective. The Sicilian, contrary to common belief, possesses a strong sense of morality; however, this morality differs in some ways from that of Italians in the north.

For example, his morality is more often expressed in private relationships rather than in the scrupulous fulfilment of public duties as a citizen. Thus, on the island, even an honourable man—regardless of any mafia influence—when faced with the dilemma of either denying the truth in court or betraying the trust of a friend or acquaintance who has confided in him about a serious matter, will almost always resolve the moral question in favour of loyalty to the friend, even at the expense of justice.

Returning to the *cosca mafiosa*, it is a simple yet solid organization, devoid of formal structures or bureaucracy. There are no formally elected presidents or secretaries, nor are there official membership lists. Leadership typically falls to three, four, or five individuals who hold greater influence due to factors such as their age, intelligence, social status, past actions, criminal convictions, and, above all, their superior experience and skill in the complex art of committing crimes with impunity. If one member stands out above the rest in a combination of these qualities, they naturally assume the role of supreme leader.

The influential members of mafia clans typically hold a social status slightly higher than the poorest segment of the Sicilian population, but it rarely rises to the level of the middle class. They are almost always small landowners, tenants of rural estates, overseers, stewards, brokers, or small-scale traders dealing in citrus fruits, livestock, and other agricultural products.

Under the guidance of these leaders operates a group of young men, typically no more than a dozen. Some, bolder, quicker, and more ambitious than the rest, pursue a life of crime in the hope of advancing their careers. They are motivated by a mix of admiration and envy for the older criminals, whom they see as prestigious figures who have achieved a social status unlikely through honest means. Others, however, are less capable—poor in spirit, half-witted, and with no future in crime. Driven by necessity, a mafia upbringing, and fear, they become blind tools in the hands of the *capi*.

In fact, it is perhaps these individuals who are the most dangerous tools, as suspicion from victims and authorities rarely falls on them. Under the fearful hypnosis of seasoned criminals, they become capable of committing the gravest offenses. There are numerous examples of such numbskulls (*microcefali*), who, once mocked by everyone, transform into terrifying hitmen. They ambush and kill multiple people with a shotgun blast to the back, often without any compensation, driven solely by the force of threatening commands and the occasional solemn slap from men known for their bloodthirsty reputation. The fear instilled in these hitmen is so strong and deeply ingrained that, even in prison, they almost never reveal the names of the masterminds behind the crimes they carried out.

The mafia *cosche* are spread throughout the rural towns of the island and the villages surrounding Palermo, with each town or village hosting one, or at most two, clans.

In cases where two clans exist, trade rivalries often lead to a series of mutual murders, typically carried out through ambushes or treacherous gunfire from behind. However, it is more common for each clan to have its own territory to exploit, avoiding interference with neighbouring clans. Relations between clans are generally cordial, based on mutual respect. On rare occasions, two or more neighbouring or distant clans may collaborate to commit a crime, particularly in cases of cattle theft.

Clans that extend across multiple towns and reach memberships of eighty to a hundred or more affiliates are extremely rare. In fact, I believe that since the unification of Italy, only four or five criminal organizations in Sicily can be cited as having grown to such an extraordinary and monstrous extent.

It is worth noting that in many towns on the island, mafia clans have never been present, while in others, they existed only briefly and struggled to establish themselves, making them easy to eradicate. In the eastern provinces, where such fortunate towns are abundant and indeed constitute the majority, violent crime is naturally much rarer.

VI.

The objectives pursued by mafia clans are numerous, but despite their diversity, they can be distilled into a single goal: to secure the greatest prestige and the highest illegal profit for the benefit of the group or its most influential members, while minimizing criminal effort and, consequently, the risk of investigation or punishment. To achieve this, they have developed a sophisticated technique of crime, which does not exclude committing heinous acts—such as ambush assassinations—when necessary to protect the organization, secure the favour of a highly influential and unscrupulous protector, or exact revenge deemed indispensable.

However, in routine matters, they not only strive to violate the penal code as little as possible but also maintain appearances that avoid deeply offending the self-esteem or even the *mafia* spirit of their victims. They operate in a way that allows the victim, who is in reality paying tribute to the clan, to deceive themselves into believing it is a voluntary gift or the equivalent of a service rendered, rather than extortion through violence.

In one of the rural towns near Palermo, or even in a hamlet on the outskirts of the city, a gentleman purchases or inherits a piece of land planted with citrus trees, vineyards, or orchards. During negotiations or on his initial visits to the property, he notices two or three local figures who, with a deference tinged with a subtle air of self-importance—something immediately recognizable—make deep bows to him and look for opportunities to exchange a few words.

One day, while visiting the property to attend to his affairs, one of these figures—usually the eldest or most authoritative—pays him a visit. The visitor extends a warm welcome and offers his services for any needs that may arise. During their conversation, he takes the opportunity to highlight the advantages and comforts of the area: the air is fresh, the walks are pleasant, and the inhabitants are courteous and hospitable. True, some people speak poorly of the place, but those are merely slanders. There might be a few rowdy youngsters, but they are reasonable and always listen to the advice of respected individuals who know how to keep them in check.

The visitor assures the gentleman that someone of his standing, who understands the ways of the world and respects others, will always be respected in return. He emphasizes that the gentleman can live without fear, come and go at any hour, confident that his property will be secure. His wife and children will be free to move about without the slightest worry, assured that no one will harm them or show them anything but respect in both word and deed.

Eventually, the time comes when the gentleman needs to sell his citrus fruits, rent out his land, or hire a guard to protect his produce. At that point, the familiar figure reappears, offering a deal or recommending the "right" person for the job. Naturally, the offer is presented as a favourable arrangement or the individual as exceptionally trustworthy and competent.

However, if the sale or rental is handled through this unofficial intermediary, the price of the goods or the rental income will inevitably be four or five percent below the true market value. Similarly, if a work contract is finalized, while the newly hired guard will excel at protecting the property from petty rural thieves, he will quietly permit the associate who secured him the job—and his mafia allies—to take a small portion of the produce for themselves.

If the new owner has remained aloof from the start or, after initially accepting the friendly and honest welcome, chooses not to conduct his affairs according to the suggestions of the unofficial intermediary offering his services, the intermediary and his associates do not completely sever their greetings but noticeably cool their friendship.

As relations cool, a series of minor inconveniences begins to arise. One morning, for example, a dozen trees or vines might be found cut down. At night, the property may be visited by petty vandals or small-time thieves who damage the crops, steal fruit, or carry off entire sacks of lemons. If the relationship deteriorates further and turns into open hostility, more serious incidents can occur: an entire vineyard might be destroyed, an insolent extortion letter—anonymous, of course—could arrive by mail or be left at the doorstep, or a rifle shot might narrowly miss the head of a truly loyal guard who genuinely works to prevent thefts and nighttime destruction.

Extreme cases, such as the murder of a loyal guard or the kidnapping and ransom of the landowner or a family member, are very rare. These high-profile crimes draw media attention and bring the justice system's focus to bear on the local mafia clan. This often leads to the arrest of its most influential members. Although the authorities frequently have to release them due to insufficient evidence, they are still held in prison for months. Some are placed under surveillance, while others are sent to forced residence. Naturally, the elders of the mafia clans dislike such disruptions and prefer to enjoy their cherished freedom and their earnings—both honest and dishonest—in peace.

This desire for a quiet life is so strong among the leaders of mafia clans that they willingly practice forgiveness and are almost always ready to reconcile with those who, after initially showing disdain or indifference to their unofficial influence, seek to restore their friendship.

For example, if the property owner who has experienced theft in the garden, had a few dozen vines cut down, or received an extortion letter contacts the associate I mentioned, warmly welcomes him, inquires why he hasn't been around lately, and then confidentially shares the damage or offense suffered while seeking his authoritative advice, the issue is quickly resolved. Initially, the associate will claim he knows nothing about it, that the situation is new to him, and will even express surprise. However, he will promise to investigate, look into the matter, and report back. In the village, he is respected and has the necessary connections to uncover the truth.

After a few days, he returns with a cheerful demeanour, claiming to have uncovered the source of the offense against the gentleman. It turns out, he says, to have been the work of some rowdy youths—a few troublemakers whom he has already dealt with. They are now deeply remorseful for their actions and humbly apologize. The helpful man assures, with the utmost certainty, that such wrongdoing will not happen again. If the gentleman wishes to show his generosity—after all, necessity or hunger sometimes drives people to err— now that the youths are ready to throw themselves at his feet, he could offer them a small token, perhaps a few hundred lire, as a gesture to lift their spirits. Youth needs its outlet, he explains, and they would bless the gentleman for his magnanimity.

The hundred lire are given, and the gentleman expresses his gratitude for the man's skill and demonstrated friendship, urging him to visit more often. The man departs, even more pleased and deferential than before, affirming that his friendship for the gentleman has always remained steadfast.

In the island's interior, mafia clans are somewhat more primitive but operate in fundamentally similar ways. Given the nature of the region and its crops, cutting down vines and trees is less commonly used to assert control over dissenters. Instead, burning crops—and occasionally forests or olive groves—is more prevalent. It is also common for large livestock, which often spend the night in the countryside due to the widespread practice of free-range grazing, to be found slaughtered in the morning. However, the most frequent and profitable crime committed by interior clans is livestock theft. In such cases, as mentioned earlier, two clans from distant towns—often in different provinces—collaborate closely: one clan steals the livestock, while the other sells it to affiliated butchers or, at times, to military suppliers.

Even in the island's interior, one of the quickest and most common ways to recover stolen livestock is to approach the head of the local clan in the area where the theft occurred. He usually feigns ignorance of the situation but promises to investigate and consult with his associates. After three or four days, if the animals have not already been slaughtered, they are often found abandoned and wandering in the territory of a nearby town. They are then returned to their rightful owner, who, of course, offers the intermediary a gift equivalent to a quarter or a fifth of the value of the stolen property. The intermediary accepts the gift, explaining that it compensates for the time spent and the trouble caused to his friends. He adds that it also allows for a small tip and a meal—perhaps a plate of pasta and a glass of wine—for the youths who made the mistake of stealing from such a respectable gentleman but later showed remorse and made amends.

In the few towns on the island where remnants of banditry still persist, protectors are often drawn from the local clans, with the bandits' activities frequently directed by these clans against individuals considered enemies. Kidnappings for ransom—crimes that are challenging to organize due to the need for numerous accomplices and are therefore relatively rare—almost always result from collaboration between a clan and several bandits, who, naturally, are the ones to execute the crime.

VII.

The police are well aware of the key members of the crime syndicates—if not all their affiliates, then certainly those who hold importance and present themselves as leaders. This knowledge does not come from the reports of professional spies, who are often unreliable, but rather from the confidences of honest individuals from various social backgrounds, which are readily obtained.

A public security officer, marshal, or carabinieri brigadier in a given area can quickly gather information about the most prominent mafiosi if they establish personal relationships and gain the public's trust by demonstrating discretion and assuring they will not compromise their sources. Once trust is established, they can easily find someone willing to provide a truthful account of the mafiosi's activities, including the exact sources of their earnings. Criminal records are a valuable aid in these investigations, as the leaders of syndicates often have prior convictions or multiple acquittals due to insufficient evidence early in their careers.

Naturally, these investigations are easier for Sicilian officials, who can instinctively recognize varying degrees of mafia involvement and sense the existence of a syndicate. In contrast, officials from northern Italy sometimes mistakenly rely on supposed informants who are, in fact, leaders of the syndicates themselves.

However, I have also known officials from northern Italy who, after a long stay in Sicily, had developed that special instinct I previously mentioned.

Prefects and sub-prefects, if they are serious and discreet individuals, can easily obtain any information they need from the local gentlemen, provided these requests are made, as they say locally, *from gentleman to gentleman* rather than in their official capacity as public officials.

In reality, knowing who is capable of committing crimes—or who is accustomed to commanding and directing the perpetrators—is of limited use in Sicily when it comes to identifying the culprits of a specific crime. For instance, if a livestock theft, vine-cutting, or ambush murder occurs, the victim, their family, and even the police may quickly and accurately suspect, or come close to identifying, who planned and organized the crime. However, locating the actual perpetrators is far more difficult. These individuals are often novice criminals with no established reputation, as the syndicate leaders deliberately keep them in the shadows. Establishing the connection between these perpetrators and the masterminds behind the crime is even more challenging.

In crimes committed by mandate, the primary legal proof against the instigator typically depends on the confession of the perpetrator. However, such confessions are almost never given by the young individuals who carry out the criminal orders of the older syndicate members. They remain silent due to their mafia upbringing, fear of material retaliation, and the knowledge that confessing would completely ruin their criminal careers, offering no hope of immediate immunity or even a significant reduction in their sentence for the crime they committed.[2]

The mafia mindset often compels victims and witnesses to stay silent about what they have seen or heard. Even if they are persuaded to share some information with authorities during the investigative phase, when face to face with the investigating magistrate, they typically retract their statements when required to testify publicly and formally before the Court of Assizes (an official court).

The authorities would undoubtedly have greater freedom to act if they could effectively apply police measures *ex informata conscientia* (based on informed judgment). Denying weapon permits, issuing warnings, and enforcing forced residence, when applied appropriately and conscientiously, could be highly effective tools against mafia syndicates. Unfortunately, their practical application is often uncertain, inconsistent, and sporadic, rendering them ineffective. This is due to interference from powerful figures who protect criminal organizations, as well as compromises and deals that sometimes occur between the police and these syndi-

2 It was the granting of such judicial immunity to the low level executioners of mafia-related crimes that caused the great effectiveness of the famous Maxiprocesso of Palermo of the late 1980s.

cates.

VIII.

This is an appropriate point to discuss the so-called *mafia in yellow gloves*: the protection extended to mafia syndicates by individuals from the upper classes, sometimes even holding political office, and occasionally by government authorities themselves.

This protection has deep historical roots. In Sicily, certain social conditions that had likely been common throughout Italy and beyond up to two centuries ago persisted well into the 18th century and mid-19th century, only slightly diminishing over time. Until 1860, Sicilian lords and nobles often interceded with authorities to prevent harsh police measures against troublemakers living near or on their rural estates. They would, of course, guarantee that these individuals would no longer cause problems. Indeed, the offenders either remained genuinely quiet or exercised greater caution in their criminal activities.

In exchange for the moral guarantee provided by the lord on behalf of the troublemakers, he was always respected. The local syndicate not only refrained from causing him any harm but also actively prevented others from doing so, offering a kind of preventive policing that was arguably more effective than the legal system. Motivated by convenience, vanity, and a lingering mafia mindset, Sicilian nobles took pride in this respect and often boasted about it to their close associates.

However, this tradition might have disappeared during the forty years of Italian rule in Sicily if the Italian public security authorities on the island had not occasionally upheld another practice from the Bourbon era: the system of transactions and compromises directly negotiated with troublemakers. The protection once offered by nobles to petty criminals has now been replaced—and even surpassed—by the more effective protection provided by deputies, mayors, or councillors on behalf of influential mafia voters or prominent syndicate members.

The Bourbon police managed to maintain a relative level of public safety with minimal effort by promising to overlook the past offenses of criminal associations and tolerating their current activities, provided no serious crimes occurred that could provoke public outrage in the areas they controlled. At times, they even went so far as to grant a form of legal authority to certain seemingly reformed criminals, expecting them to use it to protect the lives and property of honest citizens.

These and similar measures, through which order was maintained by fostering disorder, have occasionally been imitated by Italian police and prefects. It requires no explanation to show that such remedies offer only temporary and incomplete relief to the "patient" while perpetuating the underlying illness indefinitely.

A few years after the introduction of representative government in Sicily, the mafia syndicates quickly realized the significant advantages of participating in political and administrative elections. Their involvement became even more effective and active following the passage of laws that expanded the franchise, granting voting rights not only to syndicate members but also to the social classes where these members wielded greater influence and enjoyed higher prestige.

The representative system, admirable in many respects, often prioritizes organized minorities under the guise of implementing majority rule. It is easy to see that in areas where these organized minorities consist of individuals who regularly approach criminal behaviour or openly engage in it, such groups have gained electoral influence far disproportionate to their actual numbers.

Since candidates often prioritize electoral strength over the morality of their supporters, those aspiring to local administrative positions or political office—including, at times, even opposition candidates—have frequently acted as intermediaries between the police and criminals. They have lobbied on behalf of these criminals for firearm permits, the lifting of warnings, the cessation of enforced residence, and, at times, have spoken favourably to magistrates during criminal investigations. Some have even attempted to influence jurors, who, to their credit, have often resisted corruption.

Government authorities, observing candidates—whether allies or opponents—engaging in such practices, have at times opted to deal directly with the syndicates and criminals themselves to secure votes for one candidate over another. This has led to the creation, continuation, and reinforcement of a system of compromises involving bad actors, influential individuals, and government officials. This system is now the primary source of the moral decay that afflicts and overshadows Sicily.

IX.

Some argue that eradicating the mafia in Sicily requires abolishing Parliamentarism and stripping all authority from representative institutions. Others claim that the government itself cultivates and sustains the mafia in Sicily to secure a majority of deputies from the south, which it uses to suppress representation from the more civilized and educated regions of the north. I believe both views are exaggerated.

Sicily is not so corrupt that the mafia is the sole active electoral force. Determined governments, such as during the prefectures of Gerra and Malusardi, have shown that it is possible to fight the mafia relentlessly without significantly shifting votes among Sicilian deputies from government supporters to the opposition. It seems clear to me that a government that persistently, systematically, and wisely opposed the mafia and all violent groups could ultimately secure the same majority among the island's deputies as one relying on semi-tolerance of corrupt elements.

Sicilian public opinion has consistently supported authorities pursuing serious efforts at social reform and has often countered the actions of vested interests seeking to obstruct the reformative work of government officials, as was particularly evident during the Malusardi prefecture. The jury, which reflects the average sentiments of the population, has performed fairly well in Sicily over the past decades. While some Sicilian jurors may be slightly influenced by mafia connections, their verdicts in serious cases such as extortion, theft, and murder are almost never swayed by *omertà* (the code of silence) or fear. Entire gangs of notorious bandits, such as the Maurini bandits, and dangerous, bloodthirsty mafia clans, like the one led by the Amoroso brothers, have been sentenced to the harshest penalties by Palermo's jurors.

Unfortunately, for the problem to persist, all it takes is negligence—letting things slide and continuing the status quo. In contrast, addressing it requires energy, diligence, discernment, and a long, persistent effort that demands significant time—time that ministers and even officials sent to manage the island's affairs often lack.

Prefects and police commissioners in Sicily are typically there only temporarily, and their primary goal is often to avoid unnecessary trouble during their, hopefully brief, tenure. They are expected to satisfy their direct superiors, namely the Minister and Undersecretary of State for Internal Affairs. These superiors do not fail to issue orders, provide instructions, and make recommendations. Local officials are tasked with ensuring laws are enforced, municipal administrations and charitable organizations are cleaned up, troublemakers are controlled, public order and safety are maintained, friendly deputies are supported, and opponents of the Ministry are hindered in their re-election efforts.

Attempting to accomplish all these tasks simultaneously, within a few months, and without causing uproar or friction, is a daunting challenge. The official quickly realizes that breaking compromises with troublemakers to maintain public order will likely result in a temporary rise in common crimes. If he tries to combat the usual "honourable" practices of colluding with mafia factions by supporting candidates who rely solely on honest elements, he risks exposing himself to plots and slanders orchestrated against him in Rome. Should he fail, he will bear full responsibility for the failure.

In such a situation, even a slightly flexible conscience can lead him to make compromises. He will choose to focus on only part of the assigned program—specifically, the part he considers most crucial to his own well-being and career—while setting aside any moral lectures.

Thus, relying on familiar methods—the quickest and easiest—he manages his activities to ensure that the usual "honourable" candidates emerge victorious from the ballot boxes and that no serious crimes occur in the meantime to alarm the public or attract media attention. To achieve these objectives, he maintains, and sometimes even establishes, the usual relationships between authorities and troublemakers. He does this fully aware that, for the sake of a temporary result, he is worsening the underlying issues afflicting the province. However, he also knows that addressing the long-term consequences will soon become his successor's problem.

If the official is a person of strong conscience—someone who believes that his duties extend beyond serving himself and the current government to include a responsibility to society—and if he feels compassion for the region he is called to serve, he focuses his efforts on combating a single deputy who protects wrongdoers or dismantling one mafia faction he considers the most dangerous. In short, he strives to make a positive impact during his tenure by addressing some of the thorns that trouble the province. He understands, however, that attempting to eliminate all such problems would achieve nothing but staining his hands with blood unnecessarily. Even in the unlikely event of success, it would only leave future prefects and police commissioners with roses to pick.

X.

I have nearly completed my discourse without mentioning any organization that unites and disciplines all the forces of the mafia, or rather, the mafia clans. This omission is intentional, as no such organization exists. Each faction operates independently and typically does not recognize the authority of any leader outside its own ranks.

Among factions in neighbouring areas, there may—and often do—exist relationships of friendship or enmity, as I have already noted. They may respect one another, compete, or even engage in mutual destruction. However, this autonomy stems directly from the absence of any federal structure that might unite them and enforce a common standard.

For instance, members of two clans from distant provinces often do not even know each other by name or face and interact only rarely, if at all.

It goes without saying, then, that there is no general council or supreme leader (*Duce*) of the mafia in Sicily. The commonly used phrase "so-and-so is a mafia boss" simply means that the individual is on good terms with several mafia clans, which he protects to secure their support in elections or for other, less honourable purposes.

Mafia members do not use passwords or mysterious signs of recognition—and, I hasten to add, they do not feel any need for them. Those deeply imbued with the mafia spirit, and even more so those who belong to various clans, can easily recognize one another through an indefinable quality—a certain shared demeanour or attitude—that their similar habits, moral outlook, and intellectual upbringing imprint on members of different social classes and professions.

Just as an officer in civilian clothes, a traveling salesman, a labourer, or a stylish bon vivant can immediately recognize a kindred spirit in a railway carriage or on a steamboat, so too can a mafia member identify his counterpart when away from his hometown. This natural recognition among mafiosi ensures that, when the opportunity arises, they instinctively know how to speak and act in harmony, without the need for any formal agreement.

XI.

One question remains to be clarified: the role that the mafia—understood both as a rebellion against the law and as associations of wrongdoers—has played in the commission of a crime that has rightly shocked and continues to trouble Italy: the assassination of Notarbartolo. Even more concerning is the greater scandal surrounding this crime—the prolonged impunity of its perpetrators.

Specifically, do these grave events, brought to light by the publicity of the Milan trial and deeply troubling to all who wish Italy to be a truly civilized nation, stem solely from local causes—a specific malady afflicting only Sicily—or are they also the result of broader weaknesses affecting all of Italy? Is this a more widespread, if not equally severe, affliction that taints the entire country?

I believe this investigation is both necessary and timely

because, as with the physical illnesses of individuals, an accurate, clear, and precise diagnosis of a nation's moral ills is essential for any rational remedy.

Not long ago in Italy, public ignorance regarding banking matters—combined with a prevailing notion among both rulers and the ruled that the public interest aligned with the sum of a few private interests—created a dangerous environment. This notion, unfortunately, has not yet been entirely discredited. The ignorance, coupled with the moral flexibility of those responsible for ensuring that issuing banks adhered to the law and their statutes, allowed banking regulations to be semi-clandestinely, and at times even openly and systematically, violated.

For example, new banknote issuances were authorized to support struggling private businesses and banks, during which political influence became almost a legitimate qualification for obtaining favourable discounts from these issuing institutions. The banks were even tacitly authorized—or outright encouraged—to speculate on the stock market to inflate the prices of government bonds and subsidized company stocks, under the mistaken belief that this was serving the national economy.

The swindler is like the devil—you can't offer him a finger without him taking your hand, your entire arm, and dragging you to ruin. Once legality was abandoned in banking matters—whether by permission or inspiration from above—and once actions that could not be publicly admitted were allowed, the line between what was lawful and unlawful blurred. This opened the door for a cohort of wheeler-dealers and embezzlers, with representatives among businesspeople, within the banks, in local administrations, and even in Parliament, to weave an incredibly intricate web of shady deals for their own benefit and to the detriment of the issuing banks, the State, and the public. What began as indiscretions quickly escalated into forgeries, fraud, and other crimes punishable under the penal code.

Like nearly all other issuing banks, the Banco di Sicilia also faced its own assault—most notably around 1890, the year Notarbartolo was removed from his directorship for reasons still not entirely clear. However, this attack came later and was less aggressive compared to similar assaults on the Banca Nazionale and the Banco di Napoli. Moreover, it encountered stronger resistance, leaving the Sicilian bank in relatively good condition. Today, it remains our smallest issuing institution but also the most stable.

In the final days of 1892, when the economic and moral ruin caused by the errors and weaknesses of our rulers began to awaken public awareness, the men who had long criticized our banking policy—Professors Pantaleoni and De Viti de Marco—provided Deputies Colaianni and Gavazzi with evidence of abuses and illegalities committed with the acquiescence of certain officials. As it became clear that the carnival of scoundrels was coming to an end and discussions arose about accountability, as well as administrative and parliamentary inquiries, the embezzlers connected to the Banco di Sicilia recognized the danger and began devising ways to avert it.

At this point—and only at this point—the general criminal phenomenon afflicting the entire country acquired a distinct regional dimension. The nationwide corruption became entangled in Palermo with a local infection: the mafia. Notarbartolo, a highly competent and energetic man who was relentless in opposing dishonesty, posed a threat to the guilty. He was someone who could have exposed the truth to public opinion and guided justice effectively against the real culprits. And so, they decided to eliminate him.

The atrocious plot was easier to conceive and develop in Sicily than in other parts of Italy because, on the island, the spirit of the mafia and the connections between the wealthy classes and mafia clans make the idea of bloody violence emerge more readily in troubled consciences than it would in Lombardy, Piedmont, or Tuscany. There, murder provokes far greater revulsion, even among the less respectable classes of embezzlers and high-ranking swindlers.

In Palermo, it was particularly easy for some of the wrongdoers at the Banco di Sicilia, thanks to their close ties with mafia clans, to find a skilled hitman—a true master of wrongdoing—who, with incredible audacity and cold-blooded precision, planned and executed the heinous crime. It is well known that having ready and effective means to commit evil acts often becomes a powerful temptation to carry them out.

Once the crime was committed and its perpetrator disappeared, the criminal phenomenon shed its local character and regained a national significance.

No, it was not the mafia—at least, not as many imagine it to be—nor a vast and mysterious association of wrongdoers with affiliates across all social classes, supposedly enshrouding all of Sicily, that prevented the murderers of Notarbartolo from being identified and punished. A mafia clan, as it truly operates, cannot obstruct the course of justice when it is genuinely determined to act and dismantle a criminal organization responsible for a serious crime—one that leaves a strong and lasting impression on the public. Nor can the paralysis that gripped the investigating magistracy in the Notarbartolo case be explained simply by the involvement of a member of Parliament with connections to some second-rate police officer.

The good people of Milan, now astonished and searching for explanations for the apparent weaknesses and inaction of the Palermo authorities, do not need to look as far as distant Sicily to understand this grim mystery. They need only recall another trial that unfolded close to them, one that similarly exposed the prolonged impotence of the police and judiciary in taking action against high-ranking individuals involved in banking fraud. Let them reflect on the long impunity enjoyed by Filippo Cavallini.[3]

This paralysis—or rather, these obstacles—that our police and judicial authorities have faced when trying to uncover and punish crimes tied to major banking abuses can be explained uniformly across Italy. The explanation is both serious and simple: the same series of errors and failures that allowed banking crimes to proliferate has also led to their near-impunity.

This impunity arises because, around the relatively small circle of true embezzlers, there exists a much larger circle encompassing a significant portion of our political class. These individuals enabled the circumvention of laws and the commission of irregularities, often without intending to and almost without realizing it. In doing so, they became entangled in a kind of complicity with the embezzlers—a terrible bond created by shared secrets that compels both sides to protect one another.

In Palermo, surrounding the small group of murderers who planned and carried out the assassination of Notarbartolo, there was a much larger group of simple swindlers. Many of these swindlers were unaware of the murder at the time it occurred, but because of their unconfessable ties to the assassins, they were forced to aid them in every possible way. Beyond this group of swindlers was an even larger circle of those who tolerated and acquiesced to the fraud—a

3 Filippo Cavallini was a contemporary of Mosca, MP in the Italian parliament and banker who, following a litany of financial disasters escaped to South America to avoid the consequences of his wrongdoings and was only belatedly condemned.

group that, throughout Italy, has passively and even actively, though often reluctantly, supported the actions of bank thieves.

XII.

There are moments in a man's life when, having reached maturity in judgment and conscience, he looks back on the lightness and follies of his youth. Reflecting on these, he may feel a shudder as he realizes the moral violations to which his youthful escapades unconsciously led him.

Italy now finds itself at such a moment, recognizing with alarm that its indulgence toward men who were considered capable but known to lack complete honesty, and its admiration for success in politics and business—even when achieved by reprehensible means—has unconsciously led to granting semi-impunity to swindlers and even murderers.

Just as these moments of self-reflection in fundamentally honest individuals often mark the beginning of a period of renewal, during which life's duties are taken more seriously and observed more scrupulously, it is hoped that the Notarbartolo trial will mark a turning point for Italy. It should signify the end of the disastrous cycle of errors, weaknesses, and compromises that the country has endured. It is further hoped that our ruling classes, enlightened by experience, will come to understand that allowing breaches of justice and legality creates a slippery slope: such breaches can grow uncontrollably, eventually tearing apart the moral fabric of civil society.

This would be the best tribute to Notarbartolo's memory and the greatest reward for his civic virtues. Honest in life, a martyr to honesty in death, his sacrifice will have lasting value if it prompts serious analysis of Sicily's specific ills, hastens their healing, and provokes a deep moral reckoning across Italy—one that closes the sad chapter of moral cowardice through which the nation has passed.

Men and Things of Sicily

The Municipalization of Bread in Palermo in the 17th and 18th Centuries[1]

I.

At first glance, it may seem surprising that the municipalization of the bread service—an idea that, for many, symbolizes a forward-looking aspiration—was implemented in Palermo for an extended period during a time that, while not ancient, is firmly rooted in the past. Even more surprising, however, is that this historically significant event, which should have drawn the attention of scholars focused on social and economic issues, has, as far as I am aware, not yet been explored by any contemporary writers.

It is certain that the histories, chronicles, and diaries from which I have gathered the information I am about to summarize are neither obscure nor unpublished; in fact, they have been read by hundreds of people. While it is true

1 In this 1902 work, the author examines the state of the Sicilian capital by integrating economic and institutional issues into a unified analysis. The backdrop is one of societal decline, characterized by entrenched privileges and social stagnation, where the decision was even made to establish a municipal monopoly on bread sales in Palermo.

that the history of Sicily—particularly during the Spanish and Bourbon eras—is not widely known in mainland Italy, it is studied with genuine dedication by the island's natives. Many studies have focused on military and public history, private law, and the genealogy of ancient Sicilian families, but research into the conditions and customs of the common people and the historical events they participated in has not been neglected. For example, the organization of Palermo's artisan guilds, which thrived from the sixteenth to the eighteenth century, is well-known among educated Sicilians, and the 1647 popular uprising in Palermo was thoroughly documented in an excellent monograph by Isidoro La Lumia. Moreover, Sicily's economic history has not been overlooked, especially following Cusumano's work on Sicilian banks during the Spanish era and Major Perni's statistical studies of the same period.

If, then, the municipalization of bread—an institution that operated in Palermo for so long that traces of it remain in popular customs and expressions—has yet to be documented by any writer, I believe this is because the concept existed, but the terminology did not. Or rather, the terms used to describe the institution were very different from those we use today. Esteemed writers such as Di Blasi and Villabianca, for example, who wrote at the end of the eighteenth century, consistently referred to the *colonna frumentaria* (grain reserve), *partiti della tratta* (procurement contracts), and *della meccanica* (logistics)—phrases that are now almost entirely obscure. The conventional meanings of these terms, understood in their time, are neither immediately clear nor preserved in standard Italian or local dialects. Hidden behind these unusual and eclectic terms, which vaguely hinted at administrative mechanisms that had long since vanished, scholars—especially those lacking expertise in economic disciplines—have failed to recognize the thoroughly modern institution. It is an institution that has only recently entered academic discussion and that only the boldest reformers might now consider implementing.

II.

The precise year in which Palermo adopted the idea of assigning the purchase of grain, its processing, and the sale of bread as a municipal function remains unclear. An official document—though written two centuries after the vaguely referenced event—suggests that this function was already in place by 1576. Various pieces of evidence support this hypothesis, and while it is highly likely that the municipality gradually assumed this role rather than establishing it all at once, it seems reasonable to conclude that the system was fully operational in Palermo by the late sixteenth century. Furthermore, it is historically certain that by 1647 the municipalization of bread in the Sicilian capital was a long-standing practice, with origins predating the living memory of that time.

More significant is the need to examine the unique conditions of Palermitan society that led to the adoption of this institution and its persistence over centuries. To address this, I must slightly broaden the scope of my subject to briefly consider Sicily's history during the Spanish era.

In the history books commonly used in secondary schools, as well as in the works of prominent authors, the period from the late sixteenth century to the early eighteenth century—when Spain exerted direct or indirect influence over the Italian peninsula—is typically depicted as one of widespread stagnation and artistic, intellectual, and social decline for Italy. The enduring popularity of

The Betrothed[2] has further solidified this perspective in the minds of contemporary Italians, for whom the Spanish era is often remembered solely as a time of wrongdoers, plague, and famine.

This judgment is inaccurate, or at least it cannot be applied universally to the entire period of Spanish dominance in Italy.

First, to properly assess a historical era, it must be compared with the one immediately preceding it. Such a comparison quickly reveals that wrongdoers, plague, and famine were present in Italy long before the Spaniards came to power.

Second, a detailed examination of the 150 years from the mid-sixteenth to the early eighteenth century shows that, at least during the first fifty years, Italy experienced notable social progress. Legislation, though still flawed, included provisions aimed at the common good and was enforced more effectively than in earlier centuries. Certain industries became more active, private abuses of power were better controlled, many public buildings were constructed, and cities saw significant architectural enhancements and improvements in hygiene.

Additionally, numerous charitable institutions were established to support the underprivileged, and both the population and overall wealth appear to have grown. Giuseppe Ferrari, one of the most perceptive commentators on past social conditions, recognized this relative progress achieved in Italy by the late sixteenth century.

At the start of the seventeenth century, we witness not so much a regression as a stagnation in Italy and across Southern Europe, which persisted throughout that century and

2 *I Promessi Sposi*: Manzoni's masterpiece and the greatest work of Italian literature of the 19th century.

into the early decades of the next. This stagnation is a significant and defining historical phenomenon, as it occurred alongside the rapid progress of northwestern European countries: England, France, the Netherlands, and Germany.

During this time, Southern Europe was decisively left behind, creating a gap that has never been fully bridged. The roots of the current underdevelopment in Portugal, Spain, and Italy—particularly in Southern Italy—can be traced back to the hundred years between 1620 and 1720. Southern Italy, being farther from Europe's core and with fewer connections to it, felt the effects of this prolonged stagnation even more profoundly.

III.

Sicily, particularly in the latter half of the sixteenth century, enjoyed a period of relative prosperity. It was not a conquered land or a remote province but was linked to Spain through a personal union, similar to the modern relationships between Austria and Hungary or Sweden and Norway. Sicily shared a monarch with Spain, represented on the island by a Viceroy, but its finances, administration, and judicial systems were entirely independent.

The navy was also separate, and apart from a few Sicilian regiments recruited as volunteers to serve under the King of Spain—mainly in the Flanders campaigns—the Sicilian territorial army operated independently of the Spanish forces. This army was supplied by local municipalities and barons, who carried the significant responsibility of defending the island's coasts from Turkish and Barbary incursions.

During this period, the Sicilian fleet played a significant role in the great victory at Lepanto. It single-handedly defeated a Turkish vessel at Cape Corvo, repeatedly rushed to Malta's aid, and fought hundreds of small but fierce battles, sometimes along Sicily's coasts and other times off the shores of Tunisia, Algeria, and Tripoli.

Today, we tend to view Islamic civilization as a minor factor in world history. However, in the sixteenth and even the seventeenth century, while it had already lost its artistic and scientific brilliance and was descending into the fanatical barbarism it later exhibited, it still possessed formidable military strength. From the Barbary Coast and the East, it launched relentless and unceasing attacks on European civilization.

Almost every year, Sicilian warships had to patrol African coasts to thwart raids and prevent landings by Barbary pirates on Sicily's shores. During this time, Spain, Venice, and Sicily provided a crucial service to the rest of Europe, acting as barriers against the advancing Islamic forces. In this centuries-long mission, dictated by their geographical positions, they expended their finest resources.

At the start of the seventeenth century, only two medieval European constitutions remained functional: the English and the Sicilian. By the end of the sixteenth century, the Sicilian constitution had reached a more advanced stage of development than its English counterpart. The three Chambers of the Sicilian Parliament were convened regularly every three years, and their approval was required for the collection of revenues. Additionally, a permanent Parliamentary Commission, the renowned *Deputazione del Regno*, monitored expenditures and ensured that the executive power remained within the bounds of legality.

The judiciary underwent significant improvements in the late sixteenth century, with new laws—almost always driven by petitions from Parliament—frequently motivated by a concern for the public good, understood in the context of the era.

It is well known that the medieval monarchy functioned as a federation of small monarchies, corresponding to the great baronies, and small republics represented by the communes. In northern Italy, the commune itself evolved into the state. In Spain, France, and elsewhere, the rise of absolutism after the sixteenth century suppressed and absorbed these local autonomies. In Sicily, however, the monarchy, constrained by the power of Parliament, was unable to eradicate local autonomies. These local entities consistently provided the Parliament with a foundation of political strength, along with material and moral support.

Thus, while the great barons largely retained their jurisdictions, the communes—particularly the larger ones like Palermo and Messina, which were unfortunately rivals—jealously preserved their structures as quasi-autonomous republics, connected to the rest of the kingdom through a federal pact.

This arrangement is evidenced by the constitution of the commune of Palermo, which remained nearly intact until about a century ago. It functioned as a small state within the state, complete with all the organs of governance. Executive power was vested in the "*Pretore*" and six senators, who, after 1584, were selected by the Viceroy from among the noble citizens. Only on rare occasions were two senators chosen from the common people.

The judicial power was exercised by the "Corte Pretoriana," the captain of justice, and the consuls of the guilds, who acted almost as arbitration tribunals for disputes related to their respective trades. Legislative power, in turn, was entrusted to the Council of the commune, where all citizens theoretically had the right to speak and vote. In practice, however, the Council consisted of notable figures, including noblemen, clergymen, commoners, and all the guild consuls and their deputies.

The commune maintained its own assets, bank, and even its own army, which included a small permanent force and the armed guilds. These guilds, organized by trade under their respective consuls, were responsible for guarding the city walls and ramparts, which were communal property. Alongside some nobles, they formed the primary armed force of the commune, entrusted with the defence of the city and the maintenance of public order.

IV.

As Guglielmo Ferrero observed in his *History of the Greatness and Decline of Rome*, nothing is more at odds with the views and economic policies of antiquity—and, one might add, those of the Middle Ages and all centuries up to the nineteenth—than the modern import duty on grain.

In the past, countries regarded grain with a level of importance akin to that of gold. It was seen as a misfortune for either the precious metal or the essential cereal to leave the state, and efforts were generally focused on encouraging their inflow from abroad. Following this logic, it was not the importation but the exportation of grain that was restricted—often outright prohibited. Only in cases of exceptional surplus, far exceeding domestic needs, was its export temporarily permitted.

Implementing such a policy was naturally more challenging in the rare cases of countries that typically produced grain for export. This was true of Sicily, which was a grain exporter during Roman times, under the Norman dynasty, and, after the 1500s, became the natural supplier for much of Europe, thanks to agricultural improvements driven by the broader progress of Sicilian society. There was almost always a country experiencing a failed harvest, creating a temporary but urgent need for grain. This demand allowed Sicilian producers to sell their grain at highly profitable prices.

Returning to the search for the origins of the municipalization of bread in Palermo, it was in the interest of the Sicilian nobility—who, along with the high secular clergy and certain religious corporations, owned nearly all the grain-producing lands—that the export of this cereal, or "*la tratta*" as it was then called, be permitted. On the other hand, artisans, who were solely consumers of grain, were deeply concerned with preventing its price from rising. They were especially eager to shield themselves from the sharp fluctuations in grain prices which, until a few centuries ago, could triple the cost of bread from one year to the next, often resulting in devastating famines.

Each year in Sicily, a process known as the "*scandaglio*" (probing) was conducted—an assessment to determine whether grain production exceeded domestic consumption needs and whether exportation could be allowed. If the assessment was affirmative, the amount permitted for export was also determined. These statistical surveys, even today somewhat unreliable, were undoubtedly even less accurate two or three centuries ago. At that time, errors in such assessments could have catastrophic consequences, including famine and civil war.

The Viceroy, tasked annually with deciding whether to permit or prohibit grain exportation, faced constant pressure. He had to balance the demands and greed of the nobility—who dominated Parliament and held high state offices—the needs of the treasury (as taxes approved by the three chambers largely depended on export duties for grain and silk), and political prudence, which could not ignore the desperation of the armed and organized plebeians in the major cities. It is also worth noting that the Viceroy, the government, and Parliament, when convened in Palermo, operated under the constant threat of the city's fortifications, whose cannons were zealously guarded by the guilds.

Naturally, in this situation, to prevent conflict and the

recurring clash of opposing interests, a solution was devised that, at least on the surface, appeared to eliminate all antagonism. This solution was the monopoly on bread sales assumed by the municipality of Palermo. Notably, this monopoly ensured that the price of bread for citizens remained stable, regardless of fluctuations in the price of grain.

V.

It was a long-standing custom among medieval communes across much of Europe to regulate the trade of grain and other essential goods. This was achieved by setting maximum prices, prohibiting the export of necessities, or creating large reserves to be sold to citizens at cost. The latter system sometimes persisted into the early modern era, with Machiavelli commending it. He noted that in all the free German cities, the commune always maintained enough grain and firewood in public warehouses to meet the city's needs for an entire year.

A similar system appears to have been adopted by Sicilian communes from ancient times, whenever resources permitted. For example, a complaint from the Jewish community of Palermo in 1491 reveals dissatisfaction with the Senate for failing to allocate them a proportionate share of grain. This grain was evidently being resold by the commune to citizens at a favourable price.

This practice likely inspired the commune to take control of the handling and sale of bread, establishing a fixed, unchanging price for this essential commodity. This measure shielded labourers from fluctuations in grain prices, eliminating both the impact of such changes on them and their incentive to oppose the export of this staple.

The municipal bread-baking operation in Palermo, being such an elaborate system, had to be established gradually. The first municipal ovens may have been introduced to assist citizens who could not bake bread at home, as home baking required purchasing large quantities of grain directly from the commune. Over time, it was noted that when the commune refrained from raising the price of bread, artisans quietly accepted the export of grain. This practice gave rise to the custom of never increasing the price of communal bread.

However, a solution was still needed to address the significant financial losses incurred by the city when bread was sold at a much lower price than its cost during times of famine. The remedy was found in adopting a municipal monopoly on bread sales. This allowed the commune to sell bread at a price slightly above its cost during years of abundance.

I have limited myself to stating that the custom of never raising the price of bread prevailed, not only because I have found no explicit provision mandating it, but also because I have encountered some references that suggest otherwise. For instance, a notice from the commune of Palermo, published in late 1775, explicitly states that "the pragmatic laws established for the governance of the city, dating back two centuries, prescribed that the commune sell provisions in accordance with cost and expenses."

Furthermore, I note that from time to time, when the commune was heavily burdened with debt to the royal treasury, warnings came from the Court of Madrid and later from Naples, instructing the commune to sell bread at cost price. These warnings, however, were almost always ignored. On one occasion, when the Viceroy and the ministers of the royal patrimony insisted on enforcing precise orders from Madrid, one of the most violent riots in Sicilian history erupted.

It is clear that the stability of the municipal bread price was the political cornerstone of the entire system. It represented the fundamental clause of the tacit agreement between the Senate of Palermo and the city's artisans. This price stability was also the artisans' means of ensuring the consistency of their wages. In return, they accepted the arrangement that allowed the nobility and clergy to export their grain, which inevitably raised its price for domestic consumers.

VI.

However, the system was artificial and inherently flawed, and could never be perfected. Despite the commune's monopoly on bread sales, it neither dared nor managed to prevent families from baking bread privately. This right was explicitly recognized by the City Council in 1648. While it is unlikely that poor artisan families could afford to buy grain and bake bread themselves—since grain was not sold in small quantities—aristocratic households with large staffs, access to home ovens, and flour from their estates, as well as convents and monasteries with many friars and nuns, likely found it practical to bake their own bread. These groups also distributed bread as alms during times of low grain prices, which the commune depended on both to refill its grain stores and to fund its bread-baking operations. In contrast, when grain prices rose and the commune sold at a loss, private ovens were shut down. At such times, everyone relied on communal bread, leading to a significant increase in its consumption.

Other factors also contributed to this outcome. During years of severe famine, large numbers of poor people from across the island flocked to Palermo, where begging for alms was easier, and the price of bread remained stable. As a result, the commune had to feed thousands of additional people. Furthermore, the widening price gap between bread in Palermo and the surrounding areas attracted farmers from nearby regions who came to the city to buy bread. Although this practice was officially prohibited, preventing smuggling proved impossible.

The historian Di Blasi, who lived during the first half of the eighteenth century and died at a very old age in the early nineteenth century, explicitly notes that during every famine in Palermo, the consumption of communal bread increased dramatically. He attributes this phenomenon to the saying *privatio generat appetitum* ("privation generates appetite"), suggesting that grain shortages intensified the hunger of Palermo's residents. However, he also provides a more practical explanation in the surrounding passages, where he describes the Senate's measures to prevent bread from being exported out of the city. These efforts included closing all city gates except four, which were guarded by gentlemen and guild consuls, organizing patrols along the walls to stop bread from being thrown to the starving countryside, and inspecting ships and boats heading to other ports on the island or even to Naples. In extreme cases, bread was rationed, with families allowed to purchase only an amount deemed sufficient for their household's needs. This rationing system was strikingly similar to the one proposed by the swordsman Ambrogio Fusella to the unsuspecting Renzo Tramaglino, the protagonist of *The Betrothed.*

In general, the limited profits during times of abundance failed to offset the losses incurred during years of famine. Moreover, in the late sixteenth and early seventeenth centuries, the constant influx of precious metals from the Americas caused a significant devaluation of money. As a result, goods became more expensive, and the average price of grain rose substantially higher than the fixed price at which the commune of Palermo sold bread. This disparity led to considerable financial losses and, in the process, created a massive public debt. By this time, the annual interest payments on the debt alone amounted to 150,000 ounces, roughly equivalent to 1.9 million lira. At an interest rate of 5%, which was relatively low for the period, this debt represented a principal of 38 million lira—approximately 100 million lira in today's terms. This figure is staggering, especially considering that the mid-seventeenth-century population of Palermo likely did not exceed 140,000 people, and average wealth—and therefore the taxable base—was significantly lower than it is today.

To cover the interest on this debt, the authorities naturally turned to broad-based taxes, placing duties on widely consumed items such as flour for household bread and macaroni, wine, meat, oil, and cheese. In effect, the low price of bread was maintained at the expense of other essential foodstuffs. However, these measures proved insufficient during the famine of winter 1646-47, which exhausted both the grain reserves and the municipal treasury. With no credit remaining, the government was forced to impose loans, seizing money from depositors in the municipal bank and compensating them with 5% interest. The royal treasury also provided some funds, but by spring 1647, the commune faced a dire choice: either raise the price of bread or suspend payments on municipal bonds—the equivalent of today's debt coupons—to its creditors.

VII.

The crisis struck at a particularly inopportune time for the Spanish crown, which had already lost much of its military prestige and was mired in severe financial ruin. In 1640, Portugal had risen up and established itself as an independent monarchy, and shortly thereafter, Catalonia rebelled, demanding autonomy. Around the same time, a revolution erupted in Naples—known as the "Masaniello revolt"—and resisted Spain's attempts at suppression for over a year.

In the spring of 1647, the Viceroy, the Marquis of Los Vélez, fearing the loss of funds the royal treasury had lent to the municipality during the famine, pressed for strict action from the Court of Madrid. The resulting order required either an increase in the price of bread or, alternatively, a reduction in its weight. At the time, bread—sold by the municipality in uniform, fixed-weight loaves—was a staple of daily life, as it remains in Palermo today. Reducing the loaf size seemed less conspicuous and, arguably, less objectionable than raising the price.

The order arrived in mid-May, accompanied by new tax measures to bolster revenues. For instance, barley was taxed at a rate equivalent to 25% of its value, and an annual fee of 65 lire was imposed on every two-horse carriage, a sum equivalent to at least 150 lire in today's currency.[3]

For several months, the situation remained calm as everyone awaited the outcomes of the tax reforms. However, the guilds and the nobility lived in constant mutual suspicion. Tensions escalated as many nobles began retreating to their estates, which irritated the guilds, who saw this as a loss of both clientele and work opportunities.

At this point, a significant social struggle erupted between the different classes of Palermitan society. Its dramatic and colourful nature has captured the particular interest of historians. This conflict bore a striking resemblance to the well-known Masaniello revolt in Naples,[4] a tragic prelude lasting only a week, which marked the beginning of a prolonged struggle between Neapolitan commoners, the nobility, and the Spanish in 1647 and 1648.

3 800 USD.

4 Masaniello (1620–1647) was a Neapolitan fisherman who gained prominence as the leader of the 1647 revolt against Spanish Habsburg rule in the Kingdom of Naples.

The struggle in Palermo began when a goldsmith named Giuseppe D'Alessi, who had been in Naples during the eight days when Masaniello—an ill-fated fishmonger from Amalfi—rose to become the people's captain-general, witnessed those dramatic events. Masaniello was eventually killed by an enraged populace, only to be later venerated by the same people. Upon returning to Palermo and finding the city rife with tension and suspicion, D'Alessi gained the support of the tanners' and curriers' guilds, along with the common people who belonged to no trade. With their backing, he set out to emulate Masaniello's uprising.

When the revolt erupted, D'Alessi and his followers succeeded in forcibly expelling the Marquis of Los Vélez and his Spanish guard from the royal palace. Initially, the other factions remained somewhat neutral, but their sentiments were soon roused. When the humble goldsmith, now the general captain of the city, summoned the consuls to the Church of San Giuseppe, an ambitious program of democratic reforms was drafted for implementation across the entire island. This program was so extensive that it even proposed reducing land rents and confiscating uncultivated lands.

However, D'Alessi's rise to power, like that of his Neapolitan predecessor Masaniello, lasted less than a week. Though milder in temperament, the Palermitan craftsman strictly opposed looting and personal vendettas, yet he, too, succumbed to the intoxication of grandeur. In Naples, the task of undermining Masaniello fell to the Viceroy Count of Arcos; in Palermo, with Los Vélez having fled, the role was eagerly taken up by the Spanish inquisitor Trasmiéra, Don Ottavio Lanza (Prince of Trabia), and other nobles and clergy. Their efforts yielded the same results: they skillfully incited rivalry between the fishermen and the tanners, fostered jealousy among the guild consuls toward the goldsmith who now walked among princes and commanded like an absolute ruler, and orchestrated a rebellion.

One day, the fishermen, allied with the nobles and their followers, attacked D'Alessi and his main supporters in his headquarters located in the narrow streets of the tanners' district. He was killed, along with his closest allies. With his death, the democratic reforms of the Church of San Giuseppe also perished.

VIII.

The financial uncertainties facing the municipality persisted, and there was no reversal of the democratic tax reform approved by the City Council and sanctioned by the Viceroy.

Two months after Alessi's death, the Marquis of Los Velez also passed away. Historian La Lumia describes him as a pompous nonentity who was entirely unequal to the challenges of his mission. He was succeeded by Cardinal Teodoro Trivulzio, a Milanese by birth, noble in lineage, a valiant warrior in his youth, and a shrewd politician in his later years.

Cardinal Trivulzio entered Palermo without a royal military escort, relying instead on the loyalty of the honourable guilds. He summarized his program with a few familiar yet resonant words—bread, justice, and renewal. Though these phrases often conceal vagueness and duplicity, they were well received. He immediately began addressing abuses, ensured that bread continued to be sold at its old price, and left future reforms to develop in their own time.

Meanwhile, the suspension of interest payments on the municipal debt had destroyed both public and private credit, triggering a widespread crisis. Money ceased to circulate, leaving workers without employment. The new taxes generated revenue that was wholly insufficient to meet the state's needs. Even then, a principle of financial science became evident—one that remains relevant today: in poor, heavily taxed countries, much of the financial burden inevitably falls on the poorer classes.

Artisans were especially resentful of the window tax, while the nobility, affected by the highly burdensome family tax, threatened a consumer boycott and spoke of retreating to their country estates. Additionally, salaries for all municipal employees were reduced, but the savings achieved were minimal.

As public and private misery deepened, artisans began to understand firsthand that, no matter how cheap food might be, their earnings often weren't enough to buy it. Conditions became so dire that, about a year later, the consuls appealed to Trivulzio, urging him to intervene—even if it meant restoring the old consumption taxes.

The Milanese nobleman, a true statesman, avoided taking undue advantage of the situation. He replied that the old consumption taxes had been abolished by the municipal council, and it was up to the council to propose their full or partial reinstatement. Consequently, the council was convened, with about two hundred consuls and deputies in attendance. Representatives from various social classes engaged in discussions that, without excessive dominance from one side or submissiveness from the other, addressed the mutual interests of the city and its people, ultimately reaching a compromise acceptable to all parties.

The council first resolved to prevent the municipality from declaring bankruptcy. This decision was crucial not only to restore credit and revive monetary circulation but also to protect the interests of numerous creditors, including charitable institutions and families of modest means. In a move ahead of its time—anticipating reforms later introduced by Sella and Sonnino—the interest on municipal debt was reduced from five to four percent.

Several taxes were retained, including the new carriage tax, the tobacco duty, and the barley duty. However, the window tax and the poll (or family) tax were abolished. The consumption tax on meat, which had never been eliminated, remained in place, while the old duties on flour, oil, wine, and cheese were reintroduced in a somewhat reduced form. Additionally, exemptions from these duties previously enjoyed by the clergy, certain officials, and the Viceroy were abolished. Notably, the Viceroy set an example by voluntarily relinquishing his privilege.

These measures enabled the municipality to pay reduced interest to its creditors and continue the municipalized bread service. Although the price of bread rose slightly—by just over two cents per kilogram, matching the duty private bakeries paid on flour—the Senate promised to maintain this price for ten years, a commitment that ultimately lasted much longer.

With municipal finances restored and social peace reestablished, Cardinal Trivulzio earned the trust of the guilds to such an extent that he persuaded them to remove cannons from the city ramparts, where they had long threatened the royal palace. The cannons were moved to the neutral grounds of the archbishop's palace, where they remained until 1676. That year, during a naval battle in the Gulf of Palermo between the Dutch, Spanish, and Sicilian fleets on one side and the French fleet on the other, the Sicilian ship *San Giuseppe* was lost. In the aftermath of this defeat, the people of Palermo reclaimed the cannons, citing the city's need for defence. These weapons would protect Palermo's security and stabilize bread prices for nearly a century.

IX.

The major financial reform of 1648 appears to have been

successful. For a long time thereafter, there were no significant discussions about the financial difficulties related to grain supplies. The municipalization of bread was not only maintained but also expanded to include other essential foodstuffs, such as beef, olive oil, and cheese.

I do not know precisely when the municipality began expanding its responsibilities for provisioning, as historians and chroniclers of the eighteenth century generally describe it as an already established practice. With thorough research in the diaries and archives of Palermo, important details on this matter might be uncovered. It is possible that the expansion of the food enterprise was initiated to compensate the municipality for the losses incurred in bread sales. For certain goods, such as olive oil, purchasing wholesale during periods of abundance—which tended to occur almost regularly every two years—and selling retail could provide a nearly guaranteed profit.

What is clear is that price stability was extended to the newly municipalized goods. Once these goods came under municipal management, their prices no longer increased. It can be inferred that the consumption tax levied by the municipality was included in the original cost of these goods.

Until the mid-eighteenth century, the municipal enterprise managed to sustain itself, balancing losses during years of famine with profits during normal times. Additionally, it appears that currency devaluation halted by the late seventeenth and early eighteenth centuries. During this period, as the Spanish monarchy entered its steepest decline, it neglected maritime security, enabling Barbary corsairs to disrupt trade. This severely hindered the export of Sicilian grain, exacerbating public and private hardship. However, the resulting depreciation in the price of basic necessities allowed Palermo's grain administration to recover financially.

In 1713, Sicily was ceded to the House of Savoy. It was

occupied again by the Spanish in 1719 but quickly fell into Austrian hands, where it was heavily exploited until 1734. That year marked the establishment of Naples and Sicily as independent and separate kingdoms, united under the personal rule of Charles III of Bourbon. From then until the end of the eighteenth century, the two regions experienced significant intellectual, social, and economic progress.

With improved security both domestically and at sea, Sicily revived its ancient exports of grain and silk and began new exports of wine and oil. The population grew significantly, along with the wealth and value of the land. Many uncultivated areas were brought under cultivation, and a process of agricultural intensification began. Vines, olive trees, and other fruit trees gradually replaced open pastures and extensive grain cultivation.

However, alongside this growing prosperity in wealth, trade, and population, Sicily faced a challenge familiar to much of Europe in the second half of the eighteenth century: the rising cost of basic necessities, particularly grain, meat, and cheese.

In Palermo, the municipal food supply company, commonly known as the *colonna frumentaria*, soon began to feel the effects of the crisis. By 1756, no contractor was willing to supply beef at the traditional fixed prices. As a result, the municipality took over the sale of beef, becoming its direct economic administrator. It purchased cattle from Tunisia and Calabria, fattened the livestock in its own stables, slaughtered them, and sold the meat directly. This initiative, however, led to substantial financial losses.

In 1763, a famine struck, completely depleting the capital of the *colonna frumentaria*. The municipality resorted to makeshift measures and loans, which ultimately led to the sale of approximately three million in municipal assets. In 1772, the window tax was reinstated. Despite these efforts, the financial situation continued to deteriorate. The quality of food, even in the city's most exclusive shops, declined significantly and eventually became scarce. By early 1773, artisans were reduced to fighting one another for even a small piece of caciocavallo cheese.

Discontent among the common people and the honourable working class, who relied on the system of fixed prices, was immense as they saw it come under serious threat. The failure of the *colonna frumentaria* was largely blamed on poor administration, corruption among the most recent praetors and senators, their inability to stand up to food contractors and sellers, and especially the protection offered by Viceroy Marquis Fogliani to abusers, whether powerful or of lower status. This was further exacerbated by his leniency in permitting the export of grains, oils, and cheeses, as well as his tolerance of smuggling, even when such exports were officially prohibited.

X.

The Marquis Fogliani was not a grand lord or a viceroy in the Spanish tradition but rather a modest and diligent nobleman from Modena. Entering the service of the Court of Naples, he used his skills as a meticulous and attentive civil servant—knowing when and how to win the favour of his superiors—to rise to prominence. With possible support from Minister Tanucci, another influential Modenese figure in the Bourbon government, he attained the significant position of the King's representative in Sicily. The perspectives on his character differ: Di Blasi, an honest man but an official historian inclined to praise those in power, spoke highly of him, while Villabianca—a Sicilian nobleman—offered a more critical view. Villabianca, with a touch of clever insinuation, criticized Fogliani for not giving enough importance to noble birth and merit, while placing excessive trust in less capable individuals. These contrasting accounts make it difficult to form a clear opinion of the man who ruled Sicily at the time or to assess his true level of responsibility.

Overall, he appears to have been a good man and a capable bureaucrat, far superior to the typical prefects the Italian government now sends to oversee elections and, incidentally, to administer the island's provinces. According to Villabianca, Fogliani's main fault seems to have been his unusually long tenure of eighteen consecutive years in the vice-royalty.

Around every Viceroy, a camarilla would often form—a group of friends and trusted individuals who flattered, served, and simultaneously exploited him. However, because viceroys were usually replaced every three years, or at most every six, this system created a kind of rotation among the ambitious and scheming. Those out of favour could tolerate their misfortune, knowing that their chance might come with the next change in leadership.

When it became clear that this rotation was no longer being observed and Fogliani was being reappointed indefinitely at the end of each three-year term, resentment grew. The immense crowd of disillusioned individuals—those seeking positions, favours, undue influence, or leniency from the authorities—turned their anger against him. Using a strategy that remains unclear, Fogliani was portrayed to the people as the embodiment and source of all their troubles.

On 5th July 1773, the Senate of Palermo was renewed, and Cesare Gaetani, Prince of Cassero, assumed the role of praetor. He was a nobleman who, as Di Blasi emphatically highlights, had no debts to anyone, not even to the contractors of the public grain supply. Gaetani combined a genuine love for the public good with a strong desire for popularity. Upon taking office, he promptly declared his intention to combat abuses and restore the grain column.

For several months, conditions genuinely improved, thanks to the increased vigilance of the municipal authority, the absence of famine, and primarily a loan that temporarily revitalized the food supply system. Demonstrating a selflessness—though not without precedent—the praetor personally guaranteed this loan with his private assets. The goodwill Prince Cassero earned among the workers and common people of Palermo through these efforts had not yet diminished when, in September, he developed kidney stones. Following the advice and assistance of a doctor, who was the son of a servant of the Viceroy, he underwent surgery but ultimately passed away.

The public quickly became convinced of a sinister conspiracy involving the Viceroy and the entire clique of public fund embezzlers, whom they began to blame for the death of the beloved praetor. The spontaneous anger of the artisans over the collapse of the grain column and the fixed-price system for provisions was cleverly channelled and directed against Fogliani. Riots erupted, with the protesters demanding his removal.

On September 19th, the consuls were summoned by the archbishop. In response to the prelate's appeals to dissuade the people from their revolutionary intentions, they muttered under their breath that if Fogliani refused to leave willingly, they would find their own way to resolve Palermo's troubles.

The very next day, the cannons on the ramparts were once again aimed at the royal palace, and an immense crowd of armed citizens marched on the Viceroy's residence.

The representatives of the workers did not officially appear, but the majority of the insurgents were drawn from their ranks, and many consuls were among them. The palace was guarded by two royal regiments—one Sicilian and the other Swiss—but Fogliani had issued strict orders not to fire or shed blood. As a result, the soldiers were overpowered and disarmed, and the Viceroy himself was taken prisoner.

He was immediately placed in his carriage, surrounded by six consuls who used their bodies as shields to protect him from the mob's aggression, and transported to the marina. There, he was put aboard the first available boat and sent out to sea.

XI.

The situation concluded less tragically than might have been expected. The archbishop temporarily assumed the powers of the viceroy, and the city remained under the control of the labourers for a few months. During this time, bread and other provisions continued to be sold at their usual fixed prices. Minister Tanucci wrote that the King would address the events in Palermo with the heart of a father rather than that of a sovereign.

For the moment, the only demands were the return of the rifles taken from the soldiers and the execution of three or four unfortunate individuals from the lowest social classes, who were conveniently labelled as the leaders of the uprising. Meanwhile, the royal treasury provided the "*colonna frumentaria*" with an interest-free loan of more than six hundred thousand lire, effectively a non-repayable grant, enabling it to continue operations for the time being.

As a result of the crisis, a new viceroy was appointed to replace Fogliani, and the garrison was reinforced with strict orders not to allow themselves to be disarmed again. Through a mix of persuasion and threats, the consulates were compelled to relinquish the fortifications and cannons, which, according to Villabianca, the artisans valued more highly than their own wives. Gradually, and with the necessary precautions, the system of fixed quotas—or the invariability of food prices—was dismantled.

In reality, the general rise in prices made it impossible to maintain the price levels set in 1648. The six hundred thousand lire provided by the royal treasury in 1774 were exhausted within just a few years. With each new municipal contract for the public supply of meat, oil, or cheese, maintaining the old prices required substantial subsidies—similar to those still used to support managers of musical theatres.

As a result, in 1776, the municipality abandoned its monopoly on the sale of oil, allowing private individuals to compete and subsequently increasing the price of oil sold in its own shops. A similar reform was implemented for cheese in 1781. Finally, at the end of the same year, the reform was extended to bread, with its application continuing into the following year.

With the growth of capital, the intensification of agriculture, and a significant increase in the island's population—from 1,150,000 in 1714 to 1,800,000 in 1798—the entire old economy of the Sicilian State collapsed. In 1781, the government completely reformed the outdated grain export system, removing from the Viceroy's discretion the power to permit or prohibit exports on a yearly basis. This reform eliminated a longstanding source of speculation, favouritism, and abuse.

This change was just one of many measures aimed at implementing a genuine free trade policy for cereals. However, due to the increasing abandonment of fields—a consequence of the expansion of capital and labour—grain exports from Sicily ceased by the late eighteenth and early nineteenth centuries. Shortly afterward, grain began to be imported from Black Sea ports, effectively ending the primary reason for the municipal control of bread in Palermo.

During this time, political and social conditions were also evolving. Bourbon despotism adopted the principles of the French Revolution, but only to the extent that they served its interests. This led to the gradual curtailment and eventual abolition of municipal autonomy, as well as the dissolution of trade guilds. Consequently, Palermo's once-prestigious guilds came to an end, showing their final signs of vitality during the Revolution of 1820.

In 1812, there was an attempt to modernize the centuries-old Sicilian constitution to align with contemporary concepts and needs, but by 1816 it had disappeared entirely, marking the end of the island's autonomy. Sicily was subsequently divided into provinces and became an integral part of the newly established Kingdom of the Two Sicilies.

It was during this period—an era still within living memory of our grandparents—that the final traces of the municipalization of bread and other foodstuffs in Palermo can be found. After 1782, the municipality, having abandoned its monopoly and fixed pricing measures, limited its role to maintaining "comparison shops," similar to those occasionally established even today during periods of rising food prices.

Experience must have quickly demonstrated that private competition offered better goods at lower prices once the municipality stopped incurring losses to sell its own. However, even after its purpose had ceased, an organization as established and complex as Palermo's municipal food distribution company was unlikely to vanish overnight. As a result, remnants of its existence can still be traced into the first decade of the nineteenth century.

XII.

With the historical and expository section of the topic now complete, it would be highly interesting to closely analyse how the institutions managing Palermo's food supply operated, evaluate their practical flaws and merits, and draw lessons from them relevant to the modern debate on the municipalization of public services, including proposals to extend this to bread.

I must state upfront that what I have been able to determine on this subject is not particularly relevant to our purposes. This is primarily because the municipalization of that era addressed ideas, needs, and social conditions vastly different from those of today. Additionally, the details that would be most relevant to us are precisely those that historians and chroniclers omitted—not out of malice or ignorance, but because, at the time, these matters were widely known and taken for granted.

From the information I have gathered, it appears that the municipalization of foodstuffs was not unique to Palermo. A similar system operated in Messina, and in a more rudimentary form, it existed in other cities and royal towns of Sicily—those not under the control of any feudal lord. In these places, the municipality typically purchased grain in bulk during the harvest season and resold it in small quantities to citizens at cost price.

The quality of the goods sold on behalf of the municipality of Palermo must have been generally good, as I have found only a few complaints on the matter. Bread was sold in loaves weighing 925 grams each, as well as in loaves exactly half that weight. Additionally, smaller loaves were available, which cost slightly more proportionally—perhaps because they were better baked, more finely crafted, and regarded as luxury bread. Each loaf bore the municipal stamp.

This practice of selling bread in loaves of standardized weight, stamped by the baker, still exists in Palermo. Moreover, to emphasize that an item's price is well-known and fixed, people in Palermo commonly say, "It's like bread in the square" ("è come il pane in piazza").

In Palermo, beef is still sold without the bone, with the

various parts of the animal divided with anatomical precision, each assigned its own specific price. A single ox yields seven or eight different cuts of meat, a fine subdivision that appears to be a legacy of an era when the butcher's trade was heavily regulated by bureaucracy. Similarly, oil and cheese were offered in various qualities, each naturally priced differently.

The municipality managed the food supply either through direct oversight or contracts known as "*partiti*." Grain was typically procured through large, multi-year contracts, often lasting five years, where the contracted company was required to supply a fixed amount of grain annually at the same price. However, during famines, the contracted grain would fall short, necessitating additional purchases at exorbitant prices. Bread, though seemingly made and sold cheaply, required the municipality to establish special and stable contracts with the guilds of millers and bakers.

In the final decades of municipalization, privately baked bread was also permitted, provided the bakers purchased their grain through the municipality or with its involvement. These private bakeries, collectively referred to as "*la meccanica*," were reportedly sources of exploitation. They sold poor-quality bread, likely catering to the poorest, who often could not afford to pay in cash.

The sale of oil, meat, and cheese was primarily entrusted to companies of speculators, composed of both nobles and commoners. A key condition of these contracts was that sales had to be conducted at fixed prices (though I am unaware of how the municipality ensured the reimbursement of the consumption tax, which had been levied on the leased goods since before 1648).

In addition to holding monopoly rights, the leaseholders were likely granted access to municipal shops for their operations. Occasionally, as I have noted, to prevent the leases from going unclaimed, the municipality provided capital advances and other incentives to the leaseholders. Direct management of the business, however, was generally considered financially unviable.

Smuggling, an inevitable consequence of monopolies, did occur and was punishable by a fine of sixty-five lire whenever it was legally proven.

Abuses, while present, do not appear to have been widespread or severe, given that the municipalization of foodstuffs in Palermo lasted for about two centuries. It is certain that some administrators profited personally from managing the municipal enterprise. Although there were no newspapers at the time to report on such matters, these issues were clearly alluded to in satirical verses and pasquinades, some of which have survived. These works openly criticized the misdeeds of the powerful, with the anonymous authors seemingly unconcerned about the risk of defamation lawsuits.

While some administrators engaged in theft, many must have been honest, diligent, and prudent, as nobles generally valued their popularity and the good reputation of their families. Moreover, those known for corruption faced the risk of having their homes ransacked and devastated at the first sign of popular unrest.

Even during these chaotic acts of public retribution, it was customary for the crowd to smash and destroy everything without stealing even a pin. The authorities inevitably arrived only after the chaos had subsided and focused solely on preventing fires and murders.

The main flaw of the system was undoubtedly the administrators' reluctance to raise food prices, even when it was absolutely necessary. Each administration preferred to muddle through, presenting adjusted budgets, incurring municipal debts, and generally leaving the situation even more compromised for their successors, all to avoid the responsibility and unpopularity of increasing prices. This flaw should provide significant food for thought for modern proponents of municipalization, particularly given that today's municipal administrations are elective.

Finally, for those inclined to investigate further, more detailed and reliable information should be readily available in Palermo. There, one can likely still find the minutes of municipal council meetings, records of Senate deliberations, and even the texts of contracts with leaseholders. I cannot say whether, or to what extent, a detailed study of these documents would contribute to addressing the current debates over new services to be entrusted to municipalities. However, I am certain of this: such a study would cast significant light on the economic and social conditions of Palermo and Sicily from one and two centuries ago. It would illuminate the Sicily that was not merely an ancestor but the very mother of today's island—a Sicily from which modern times have inherited its vital essence, moral and intellectual traits, faults and virtues, and all the unique characteristics that continue to distinguish it from the regions of northern and central Italy.

If the goal is truly to revive the South (the Mezzogiorno), the first step is to understand it. For this purpose, no study is as valuable as an examination of the last centuries of its history. Moreover, since we tend to love and appreciate what we have worked hard to understand, research into the municipalizations of Palermo during the seventeenth and eighteenth centuries may foster mutual sympathy between the island and other regions of Italy. Such understanding will likely contribute to Sicily's moral, intellectual, and economic revival—a task that will undoubtedly define the twentieth century.

The Palermo Inquiry

I.

The Palermo inquiry[5] was neither conducted nor initiated by the Government or Parliament but rather by the City Council. It was launched to investigate the truth behind rumours—primarily spread through socialist newspapers—concerning the misconduct and neglect of those managing the municipal affairs of Sicily's principal city. These rumours gained traction due to the poor and steadily worsening state of the city's finances.

I will state upfront that the inquiry was thorough. Reading the three substantial volumes of its findings provides not only a detailed understanding of the unfavourable conditions of the Municipality of Palermo but also identifies the root causes of its current misfortunes. Furthermore, the report specifies the personal responsibilities of the mayors, councillors, and employees entrusted with the city's admin-

5 The 1894 trial in Palermo followed the Sicilian peasant uprisings of 1893–1894. To suppress dissent, the Italian government prosecuted those involved in the protests with harsh sentences. This trial highlighted the tensions between the government and the working class in southern Italy, particularly in Sicily, where social and economic inequalities were severe.

istration over the past twenty years.

It is important to note that an inquiry is, by its nature, an act of criticism—a search for faults, including omissions—rather than a balanced judgment weighing both merits and demerits. Indeed, the inquiry's final pages emphasize the significant challenges faced by Palermo's administrators as they attempted, over twenty years, to guide their city along a path that northern and central Italian cities had traversed in half a century. While this acknowledgment does not fully excuse their actions, it does somewhat lessen their moral responsibility and may lead public opinion to consider, at least in some cases, mitigating circumstances.

It is also worth noting that, because the inquiry focused on the elective administrations, it does not address any errors made by the royal commissioners who governed the municipality of Palermo on three occasions, even though it is unlikely they were entirely infallible. For the same reason, the five dedicated individuals who, with true self-sacrifice and great civic courage, exposed Palermo's municipal failings only briefly and in very general terms referred to the responsibilities of the (unelected) supervisory authorities. These authorities could have prevented many of these failings by enforcing compliance with existing laws and regulations.

II.

With this in mind, and turning to an examination of the inquiry, I believe that the many issues, flaws, and failings it revealed in the municipal administration of Palermo can be grouped into three distinct categories. The first involves the conduct of certain municipal councillors and assessors—mainly professionals and, in some cases, gentlemen who had fallen into financial ruin—raising the unavoidable suspicion that they may have derived personal benefits from their administrative roles. The second concerns the selection, competence, and intellectual and moral deficiencies of municipal employees. Finally, the third pertains to the various gratuities, subsidies, and handouts that have effectively turned the Municipality of Palermo into a charitable institution—one that is not always enlightened and not always impartial.

The first group, fortunately, includes only a few cases. The most common involves municipal councillors who practiced as lawyers and had among their clients companies contracted to provide public services. These companies were often involved in disputes with the Municipality, which frequently resulted in settlements reminiscent of those that, at one time, gave the Ministry of Public Works in Italy a poor reputation.

The most serious and representative example of this kind involves a municipal councillor who served as the permanent legal representative for the company contracted to supply drinking water to the town of Scillato.

A question of incompatibility arose regarding this councillor. A Commission appointed by the Council to investigate the matter concluded that no incompatibility could be identified, as it was not explicitly defined by law. However, the rapporteur for this Commission was another municipal councillor who, like the first, was a lawyer representing a different company involved in litigation with the municipality.

Despite the favourable report, the initial vote on the issue yielded an uncertain result: twenty-five councillors supported the rapporteur's conclusions, twenty-four opposed them, and one abstained. However, a second vote held several days later resulted in a majority decision rejecting the incompatibility claim.

The Inquiry Commission later expressed regret that the councillor's actions, now legitimized, were "continuous, persistent, and vigorous" in support of the company he represented. He even publicly criticized two municipal employees who had zealously defended the town's interests in dealings with the water supply company.

III.

Addressing the second set of issues, the Inquiry Commission found it alarmingly common for employees of the Municipality of Palermo to neglect their duties or to lack the intellectual competence and moral integrity needed to perform their roles effectively.

The root of this significant problem lies primarily in the failure to follow organizational regulations, which stipulate that in Palermo, municipal employees should be hired exclusively through competitive examinations. Instead, nearly all employees have been appointed based on recommendations from mayors, aldermen, or municipal councillors—in other words, through favouritism. Unsurprisingly, the most effective "qualification" for securing the favour of these elected officials has been contributing to their election campaigns.

In Palermo, as in other cities in Southern Italy, there exists a social class that has no exact counterpart in Northern Italy and could be described as the very petty bourgeoisie (*piccolissima borghesia*). This class is so financially constrained that it almost never completes any course of study, making it ineligible to compete for government positions. Opportunities in industry or commerce are scarce, as these sectors are underdeveloped in the south, and this class is generally unwilling to take up manual labour.

For these individuals, a municipal job is seen as paradise on earth. Over the past decades, electoral canvassing—soliciting votes for their candidate by pestering relatives, friends, and acquaintances—has proven marvellous for obtaining such jobs. The slightly more educated among these job-seekers have also turned to writing for small, occasional local newspapers, where they shamelessly praise or maliciously attack candidates, depending on the circumstances. Even after securing their positions, many of these "errand boys" did not abandon their old practices, to the extent that municipal offices became populated with numerous electoral fixers and editors of local pamphlets.

It is easy to see how a councillor, having risen to his position partly through the support of his subordinates, could not enforce strict discipline among them. As a result, over time, a culture of laxity and negligence took hold in all public services, fully explaining the poor management of the municipal administration.

IV.

It remains to address the abuse of rewards, subsidies, and alms.

Palermo has spent six or seven percent of its annual budget on charity—an expenditure certainly excessive, both in relation to that of other Italian cities and even in absolute terms—given that the municipal authority, especially if elective, is not the most suitable body for distributing charity to those in need.

It is certainly necessary to recall that the private charity institutions in Palermo are poor—simply because the region itself is not wealthy—and so the municipality must cover the costs of certain services indispensable in any civilized city. However, it is also true that, while part of the municipal charity budget went to these services and to the truly destitute who were incapable of any work, another portion was used to alleviate the economic hardships—undoubtedly significant, yet still relatively minor—of that singularly small middle class already mentioned.

In Turin, the Opera Pia di San Paolo, a church-backed

charity organization, allocates part of its revenues to assisting the so-called "ashamed poor." This term refers to individuals from families who, due to their social status, feel unable to beg or visit charitable institutions. In Palermo, however, where no such institution exists, the responsibility for aiding this group has not been assumed directly by the Municipality. Instead, it has fallen—at the Municipality's expense—to mayors, aldermen, and municipal councillors.

Unfortunately, human weakness has led to favouritism in the distribution of subsidies, with a preference for friends, particularly those who supported the benefactor's election. The Inquiry Commission found that donations consistently increased during municipal election periods. Additionally, a review of the published beneficiary lists—exposed without mercy during the inquiry—reveals that many recipients are neither genuinely poor nor, much less, ashamed.

V.

At this point, one may ask: what are the remedies?

A distinction must be made between temporary remedies, which only serve to mitigate the problem for a time, and radical remedies, which would truly restore the afflicted. Among the former, the dissolution of the Municipal Council stands out—an inevitable consequence of the courageous inquiry. It is certain that in three or four months, when the voters of Palermo go to the polls, they will sweep away the corrupt or overly weak councillors, since honest citizens there are not just an isolated oasis, and the vast majority of people live by working hard rather than by currying political favour or begging for jobs and subsidies. In place of the old guard, an honest and relatively energetic administration will be established.

But one must not be under any illusions. These outbursts—these reactions from the vast honest majority of the electorate, similar to the one that occurred a few months ago in Naples—represent a great but fleeting force.

It is therefore necessary to also rely on restorative measures that act more slowly but are more reliable. These measures would include greater oversight by the supervisory authority, a slight modification of the regional character, and an increase in honest and productive work, thereby leading to greater wealth earned through honest means.

On the first point, there is no need for further elaboration. Regarding the second, however, I believe it is worth noting that the judgment or prejudice attributing a generally low moral standard to Southerners is unfounded. In my view—particularly with respect to Sicilians—their moral sense expresses itself in ways that differ somewhat from those of Northern Italians. The key difference lies in that Sicilians tend to feel a stronger sense of duty and loyalty toward individuals—be they relatives, friends, acquaintances, or colleagues—rather than toward abstract entities such as the public, an idea, a political program, or, ultimately, a collective body like the municipality or the State.

This way of thinking, while not without its positive aspects—such as the fact that the state of siege in 1894[6] left behind almost no trace of personal animosities—also has significant drawbacks. For instance, it is certainly one of the main reasons why there are no truly organized political parties in Palermo, except perhaps for the emerging socialism on the island.

Although moderate, progressive, and conservative Catholic political tendencies exist, almost no one hesitates to include a candidate with opposing political views on their Municipal Council list if that candidate is a personal friend.

6 Declared on the whole island by the Italian government in response to the peasant uprising.

This practice, by elevating personal relationships as a key factor for electoral success, fosters an environment where patronage and political cronyism can thrive.

This mindset underlies the previously mentioned cases of municipal councillors who also acted as lawyers for businesses in disputes with the municipality. These individuals were not fully aware of the delicate nature of their position, nor did their colleagues bring it to their attention.

A more effective remedy would be a stricter interpretation of municipal law, prohibiting professionals involved with companies engaged in business relationships or conflicts of interest with the municipality from serving on the Municipal Council. However, implementing such a measure without negative repercussions would require Palermo to undergo a broader political and economic transformation—specifically, becoming a prosperous and wealthy city like Milan or Turin.

Currently, the Municipality is, unfortunately, almost the only wealthy entity in Palermo, around which the majority of major business activities revolve. As a result, indiscriminately enforcing the aforementioned state of incompatibility in all cases would effectively amount to a partial ostracism of the professional bourgeoisie—a class that presently supplies the most active, intelligent, and educated members to the administrative magistracies.

Only with the growth of private industrial and commercial enterprises can a sufficiently large class of educated and capable citizens emerge, allowing for the selection of individuals without business ties to the municipal administration. Only the expansion of private employment can curb the petty bourgeoisie's desperate pursuit of municipal jobs. Finally, only with the spread of prosperity across all classes will the number of citizens increase who, free from personal interests, will consistently monitor public administration affairs, thereby strengthening voter oversight of elected officials.

Thus, the inquiry into Palermo—though the issues in the Sicilian city are less severe—ultimately leads to the same conclusion as the inquiry into Naples: the administrative and even political recovery of the Mezzogiorno is inextricably linked to its economic revival.

Palermo and the Pro-Palizzolo Agitation[7]

I.

In northern Italy, it has caused considerable dismay to learn that in Palermo, a committee has been formed, and large gatherings are being held to advocate for the innocence of Raffaele Palizzolo. This is particularly striking because the committee and these meetings clearly reflect sentiments and ideas widely shared in Sicily. The public in Milan, Turin, and Bologna had certainly expected something very different, as it was, and still is, widely believed in these cities that the conviction of the former deputy for the Palazzo Reale constituency marked the first serious blow against the mafia and that the jury's verdict aligned with the general sentiment of the population.

I will say from the outset that the difference in perspectives—the antithesis that once again emerges between northern and southern Italy—does not imply that Palermo

7 Raffaele Palizzolo was an Italian member of parliament and banker from Sicily, notoriously linked to various mafiosi. He was indicted as the instigator of the February 1, 1893, murder of Emanuele Notarbartolo, a political rival.

or all of Sicily is dominated by the mafia and Palizzolo's allies. Instead, it stems from the fact that this figure—who can certainly be described as such, given how much discussion he has generated—presents himself in two contrasting ways. One is the image perceived by the population of northern Italy, who know him only through the details revealed during the two lengthy trials and what has been reported in the newspapers. The other is the image vividly remembered by his fellow citizens. For now, let us focus on the latter.

II.

While the "Palizzolo type" is primarily a southern phenomenon, shaped by nuances unique to the regional context, it is not exclusive to the Mezzogiorno. Raffaele Palizzolo was a man who, despite lacking notable education or exceptional achievements, having no prominence in wealth creation or the liberal professions, no great fortune, and no affiliation with any political party, managed to enter public life and achieve success through sheer energy, audacity, and—one must acknowledge—unapologetic self-confidence.

He began to make his presence known a few years before 1870. This was still the golden age of the representative regime, a time when the Municipality of Palermo was hotly contested between democrats and moderates. These two groups also competed for control of the city's electoral districts, but their rivalry was limited to differing political or administrative programs and expressed primarily through newspaper articles.

Palizzolo was perhaps the first in Palermo to master the art of winning voters' support through personal favours. By skilfully applying this approach and capitalizing on the widespread discontent—which was immense at the time, and broadly concealed under the term regionalism—he successfully secured a seat on the municipal council and eventually rose to the position of alderman.

The expansion of suffrage in 1882 made it easier for the future convict to achieve electoral victories. From that point on, he was almost always a deputy—first representing the rural district of Caccamo and later the Palazzo Reale district, the most populous in Palermo. This district was dominated by the small bourgeoisie, workers, minor suburban property owners, as well as smugglers and troublemakers. After becoming a deputy, he was showered with honours and high-ranking titles. He became a permanent member of the municipal and provincial councils, the Charity Congregation, the administration of various charitable institutions, and the Council of the Bank of Sicily. Everywhere he was present, active, and vigilant—always working in favour of his friends.

When I once read a Pompeian graffiti electoral notice, which included various praises for the candidate, the words "*sustinet amicos*" ("he supports his friends") stood out. It immediately brought to mind the honourable Palizzolo.

The "friends"—primarily his voters but not exclusively—received his support in every conceivable way, with his assistance tailored to the specifics of the case, the request, and the importance of the person making it. He granted an astonishing number of favours, ranging from the trivial to the significant, both lawful and unlawful. In a single day, he might secure a gun permit for a troublemaker, arrange an undeserved bonus for a municipal employee, place an orphan in a charitable institution, or expedite a matter that bureaucratic delays would otherwise have stalled for another six months. When a matter could not be resolved, he offered promises, hopes, and kind words instead.

He was immensely popular, if popularity means being readily accessible to people of every class, rank, and moral standing. His house was open to all, whether honest individuals or scoundrels. He welcomed everyone, made promises to all, shook hands with everyone, and engaged tirelessly in conversation. He shared his poetry with all, recounted his oratory triumphs in Parliament, and skilfully hinted at the breadth and power of his connections—boasting of close relationships with ministers and prime ministers, and even implying that he enjoyed the special favour of His Majesty the King himself.

Thus, partly satisfied by his assistance, partly enchanted by his extravagant promises, somewhat entertained by the theatricality of his speech, gestures, and grandiose boasts—though they always took these with a grain of salt—and a little flattered by the opportunity to walk beside him through the city streets, many voters in Palermo, especially from the petit bourgeoisie and lower classes, became ardent supporters of Cavaliere Palizzolo, as they preferred to call him, preserving his noble title. In the Palazzo Reale district, he enjoyed an unshakeable electoral base that consistently secured his success without the need to buy a single vote. While a few of his friends were undoubtedly crafty scoundrels, the majority were individuals of limited education, average intellect, and modest morality—people incapable of serious wrongdoing but who accepted the world as it was and sought good, in the form of help and favours, wherever they could find it.

III.

He was not, in any case, without enemies and opponents. As mentioned earlier, he was not affiliated with any political party or a member of any political society, whether public or secret. Political parties, even when they occasionally allied with him, always regarded him with suspicion. The socialists were consistently fierce in their opposition, while the clerical forces only occasionally showed him favour, as he appeared to be a devout believer and extended favours to priests when it suited him.

He was also an adversary of many aspiring public officials, who viewed him as a formidable competitor—a man who held too many positions and exerted excessive influence. Moreover, he antagonized the city's most intelligent, cultured, and honest citizens, who rejected the idea that the role of a public figure was to distribute favours, often illicit, to private individuals.

Even the most upright Palermitans, including those who held him in low regard and suspected him of dubious—and likely worse than dubious—associations, did not believe him capable of engaging in outright criminal acts. It was also widely acknowledged that his carelessness and loquacity made him an unlikely confidant for true criminals, who would hardly entrust him with their secrets. If a Palermitan ever referred to Palizzolo as the head of the mafia, it was only metaphorical, as everyone in Palermo knows the mafia has no single leader. Rather than being a leader, he was a tool exploited by certain gangs of scoundrels and criminals in the outskirts of Palermo who, under his protection, could at times evade strict police scrutiny.

It was widely acknowledged that he did not derive significant financial profit from his public life. While he may have been involved in some business dealings, he was never what one would typically call a "businessman." He performed countless personal favours without ever accepting monetary compensation in return, which was one of the key reasons for his popularity.

The primary vice, the dominant passion of Raffaele Palizzolo, to which he sacrificed everything, was an infinite, boundless, and morbid vanity. For this reason, I believe that twelve disinterested and virtuous Palermitans—chosen from among those who were always too ashamed to seek favours from Palizzolo and who kept their distance from him—would require more than vague indications to conclude that his association with certain criminals had so corrupted his character as to lead him from frivolity, vanity, and intrigue to outright atrocities. Specifically, they would need convincing evidence to believe he directly and knowingly participated in the brutal murders of Miceli and Notarbartolo.

IV.

In Bologna, however, he was convicted; the public there applauded the verdict, and the popular sentiment across northern Italy certainly approved of it. This was because they believed that, in condemning Palizzolo, they were striking at the so-called high mafia—the "mafia in yellow gloves"[8]—whose influence was thought to dominate both public and private life in Sicily. This same mafia was believed to have planted false clues and evidence against the accused in the Notarbartolo murder and to have obstructed the work of the police and judiciary for many years.

I do not wish to suggest that the conscience of the Bologna jurors was influenced by these opinions about Sicilian affairs, but it is undeniable that such views played a significant role in shaping public opinion in northern Italy regarding the Notarbartolo trial. It is also clear that these opinions are, if not entirely unfounded, at least partially so, and bear more resemblance to legend than to truth.

This is common knowledge in Palermo, where it is well understood that a vast criminal organization called the mafia does not exist in Sicily. Instead, the term has been collec-

8 Yellow gloves being, in the late 18th century, attributed to the more refined social classes.

tively applied to numerous small groups of criminals, none of which has the power to paralyze the work—not of the government, nor even of a single police commissioner determined to act decisively. Sicilians recall how many times, without much publicity, members of these groups have been sentenced to life imprisonment by the courts of Palermo, Trapani, and Girgenti. They are therefore convinced that if the authorities appeared weak in pursuing the perpetrators of the Notarbartolo murder, it was not due to the influence of the local mafia, but rather for reasons similar to those that, until recently, caused financial crimes throughout Italy to be punished both belatedly and leniently.

It is now easy to understand how the inaccurate perception of Sicilian affairs that took hold in northern Italy during the Notarbartolo trial—along with the somewhat distorted view of the main defendant's character—has significantly aided the popular movement currently being promoted in Palermo by Palizzolo's supporters. This mistaken perception has also made it much harder for honest and sensible individuals to take a firm stand against this movement.

V.

I will not go so far as to claim, as others have, that forming a Pro-Palizzolo Committee amounts to defending wrongdoing. However, it is certain that such a Committee must act solely through legal channels. To begin, it may engage the best lawyers in Italy to argue for any grounds of nullity that might exist in the Bologna trial. If the Court of Cassation upholds the verdict, the Committee can then work to initiate a review of the trial.

It is important to remember, however, that obtaining a retrial first requires the identification and conviction of the real murderers of Miceli and Notarbartolo. Therefore, it is crucial to achieve complete clarity regarding those two grim events, and for that clarity to definitively establish that Palizzolo had no involvement in either crime.

It is said that, in the case of Miceli's murder, the true culprits' names are already being whispered in Palermo. However, uncovering the full truth about Notarbartolo's assassination is far more challenging. This crime was undoubtedly conceived by individuals of high social standing, characterized by their dark and secretive nature—people who act with ruthless brutality and speak only when absolutely necessary. If they were not the direct perpetrators, those who carried out the act must have been chosen from the ranks of old mafiosi, true masters of criminality, who remain silent at all costs—silent as the graves of their victims.

Yet, when an entire population decides to open its eyes, it becomes unlikely that, among so many thousands, someone will not provide a clue or lead in the right direction. After all, the number of people who could reasonably be suspected of plotting Notarbartolo's assassination is no more than four or five, and they are easily identifiable—if one dismisses the fanciful idea that the former director of the Bank of Sicily was killed out of revenge for past wrongs and instead considers the interest certain individuals may have had in eliminating him to prevent future harm.

Since it is widely believed in Sicily that Palizzolo, even if guilty—and setting aside the question of the actual perpetrators—is not the only party responsible, the agitation now stirring in Palermo could signal the beginning of the end of the dark mystery surrounding the brutal death of one of Palermo's greatest gentlemen. This unresolved tragedy continues to cast a sinister shadow over the entire Sicilian region.

In the meantime, as efforts continue to uncover the true murderers of Notarbartolo, the members of the Pro-Palizzolo Committee—and especially the good citizens of

Palermo—should remember that the former deputy of the Royal Palace, even if unjustly convicted, cannot become the symbol or banner of a movement that claims to rehabilitate a supposedly slandered Sicily. Palizzolo may be considered a martyr, if one wishes, but the Church teaches that martyrdom alone is not enough to make a saint; it also requires a lifetime of practicing heroic virtues. Moreover... even if he were canonized, I would never choose the convict from Bologna as the patron of my city.

Why the Apotheosis of Palizzolo Offends Morality

I.

The Albergheria district, the most populous neighbourhood in Palermo, is now gaining a level of national attention it had never previously sought—surpassing even the fame of the Kalsa district, which, after all, produced notable figures such as Giovanni Meli, Giuseppe Ferrara, and Michele Amari. This newfound renown comes from the fact that Albergheria is the urban heart of Raffaele Palizzolo's historic constituency. It is now preparing not only to celebrate his acquittal with great fanfare but also to return him to Parliament.

Albergheria is not, as a northern Italian newspaper recently claimed, the nest or headquarters of the Mafia, whose supposed tentacles stretch across all of Sicily. The true Mafia organizations—the *cosche*—are located elsewhere. At most, a few such groups may exist, but not within the urban core of the constituency; rather, they are found in the suburban villages annexed to it. These groups certainly do not seek attention—they make no noise and hang no celebratory lights. At most, they quietly prepare to vote for Palizzolo, but only once they are convinced that he can regain enough influence with the police commissioner to help them obtain gun permits or ease certain restrictions.

The real, authentic Albergheria—the one now lighting up its homes, cheering in the streets, preparing a triumphant welcome for the former defendant on August 2, and pressuring the honourable Di Stefano to yield his seat to his predecessor—is composed of a mix of petty bourgeois citizens, many of whom owe their modest positions in the municipal administration or in other public and private enterprises to Palizzolo. It includes small artisans, for whom he often interceded with local authorities after a brawl or with charitable organizations during times of hardship, as well as small shopkeepers who frequently depended on his help to have minor municipal infractions overlooked.

Albergheria is home to a teeming crowd of moral mediocrities, among whom are more than a few shady characters—and even some genuine scoundrels. These individuals were a constant presence in the house of the honourable Palizzolo, seeking favours and taking comfort in his grand promises and the familiarity with which their district's deputy treated them. After all, Palizzolo was the important man who, as he claimed, was on a first-name basis with the Prime Minister and even enjoyed the special favour of His Majesty the King.

II.

Ultimately, then, this is not a phenomenon unique to Palermo or Sicily, but one that can be observed throughout much of Italy—and at times even in the north. It is one of many instances where a deputy remains unshakably secure in their constituency because a series of personal favours—carried out using resources obtained through both lawful and unlawful interventions in public administration—has earned them the lasting gratitude of their voters.

Indeed, while in Sicily the phenomenon may take on a more repugnant character—more at odds with civil society due to the occasional protection extended to real criminals—the case we are examining appears, on the whole, somewhat less disturbing, thanks to a certain humorous quality woven through it. This humour faintly recalls the immortal figures of Tartarin and Numa Roumestan. Between the patron and his clients, there is more than just an exchange of favours for votes; the former flatters the vanity of the latter while also seeking their applause.

It is also worth noting that the vast majority of Palizzolo's supporters have always believed in his innocence regarding the crimes attributed to him, if only because they knew well his inability to keep a secret.

That said, it is essential to present another side of the matter—one so significant that it demands not only Albergheria but all of Palermo to reflect seriously on the consequences of the apotheosis now being prepared for Raffaele Palizzolo.

III.

This man was found guilty of commissioning a murder by the jurors in Bologna (in 1902), while those in Florence (in 1904) acquitted him by a vote of eight to four—including two blank ballots, which were, by procedure, counted in his favour but clearly reflected significant uncertainty in judgment. Even more troubling, in my view, is that the Chamber of Deputies—where he had served for nearly twenty years, and which is typically fiercely protective of its own—authorized his arrest and trial through an exceptional procedure, almost unanimously and within just a few hours, with hardly any of his colleagues speaking in his defence. Finally, he was—and to some extent still is—regarded in northern and central Italy as a mafia boss and, as such, if not the direct perpetrator, then at least the instigator of Notarbartolo's murder.

There is much that is false in this last judgment, as I pointed out following the verdict in Bologna. However, just as I then felt it my duty to present to the Italians of the North the true moral character of Palizzolo, I now feel equally compelled to explain to my fellow citizens in Palermo the reasons behind the exceptional aversion that our compatriots in northern Italy—across all political affiliations and social classes—have shown toward Palizzolo and his circle. This aversion, which fairness, a sense of justice, and the lack of conclusive evidence have only recently and with great difficulty begun to dispel, deserves careful and serious reflection.

I will therefore say, first and foremost, that the vanity and shallowness of the former deputy from Albergheria—the almost theatrical, artificial, and insincere quality present in all his words, gestures, and even his physical appearance—perfectly match the image that has taken shape in northern Italy of the mafia and its members, particularly those of the so-called "mafia in yellow gloves."

The trials held first in Milan, then in Bologna and Florence, only served to reinforce this preconceived notion. Certainly, little or nothing could be definitively proven against the defendant in the murders of Notarbartolo and Miceli, but the man presented himself in the worst possible light—if not a criminal, then at least a protector of criminals, and even suspected of having ties to brigands. I would go further and say that, over the course of those grim judicial proceedings, all of Sicily was put to shame. Its flaws, its wounds, and the weaknesses of its public and private life were laid bare, scrutinized—at times passionately exaggerated, at others casually dismissed. And throughout those long years of public turmoil, Palizzolo came to embody and personify the least admirable aspects of the island that had given him birth. Some of this was unfair—but much of it was not. His name became, in large part justly, the symbol of the moral ills afflicting the noble island.

IV.

The citizens of Palermo could legitimately take an interest in the convicted man if they believe him to be innocent—after all, even someone worse than Palizzolo should not be imprisoned for a crime that has not been proven. And, to be fair, enjoying undeserved success for many years does not justify suffering undeserved misfortune. However, once everything that could reasonably be hoped for has been achieved, it is inappropriate to prepare celebrations and triumphal arches for a man whom all the sound and upright elements of Italy regard as possessing only mediocre moral character.

It is also unacceptable to send to Montecitorio,[9] as a representative of Sicily's interests and dignity, a man who, after twenty years in Parliament, was at the very least suspected by his peers of being capable of orchestrating the assassination of Emanuele Notarbartolo. And this becomes even more unacceptable given that, after all this time, the murderers of a man whom not only Sicily but all of Italy admired for his exceptional integrity and elevated moral character remain unidentified and unpunished.

The triumph of Palizzolo and his return to the Chamber of Deputies can truly be desired and supported only by Albergheria—and by this, I mean the circle of loyal followers and admirers of the former defendant from Bologna and Florence. Palermo as a whole cannot align itself with this

9 The seat of the Italian parliament.

triumph; it cannot allow its sister cities to believe that the moral capital of Sicily is nothing more than an extension of Palizzolo's world—a grand Albergheria.

If it chooses to, Palermo can defeat the Palizzolian faction even in the very constituency where it has most deeply entrenched and fortified itself, and it is to be hoped that it will. Otherwise, the city risks losing something it holds more dear and sacred than its own material interests—something that is, in fact, the best safeguard of all public interest: it risks losing its respectability.

The *Galantuomini*

I.

The recent tragic events in Grammichele[10] have once again drawn public attention in Northern Italy to the affairs of Sicily. In trying to understand the root causes of the outbreaks of popular unrest that occasionally erupt in the island's rural municipalities, much has been said—and continues to be said—about its economic conditions. This discussion is far from pointless; indeed, although numerous studies over the past decade have examined and published findings on the causes of poverty in our southern mainland and islands, those findings are still not widely known.

It must not be forgotten, however, that Sicily's economic problems—like those elsewhere—are closely tied to broader moral and social issues. For example, the island's poverty has significantly influenced the formation and persistence of a

10 On 16 August 1905, a procession of peasants and members of mutual aid societies passed through the main square of Grammichele. The demonstration quickly spiralled out of control, and the crowd stormed the town hall, setting part of it on fire. The protesters aimed to destroy tax records, which they saw as symbols of their economic hardship and exploitation. Fourteen people lost their lives, and seventy were wounded as a result of the uprising.

particular kind of ruling class, one markedly different from the equivalent class in the Po Valley.

In turn, this unique governing class shapes not only the political and administrative life of the region but also the functioning of its economy. This, of course, illustrates one of the most consistent patterns observed in social phenomena: an effect often becomes a cause, and the cause, in turn, becomes the effect.

II.

In Sicily, as in nearly all parts of Italy, the class that forms the backbone of society—the one that elects deputies, staffs local administrations, and drives economic production, whether effectively or not—is the middle class. In Sicily, it is known as the *ceto civile* (civil class), and its members are commonly referred to by the title *galantuomini* ("gentlemen").

The other term, *cappelli* (literally "hats"), is used almost exclusively in rural municipalities and carries a slightly sarcastic tone, which makes it somewhat derogatory.

Given that the island is vast and nearly as populous as Lombardy, it naturally displays considerable variation in its social conditions and, consequently, in the makeup and mindset of its ruling classes. Even if we set aside the three major cities—Palermo, Messina, and Catania—there remain notable differences between the *galantuomini* of the eastern and northern coasts and those of the interior. For now, however, it is more appropriate to focus on the latter, who inhabit the region of the *latifondo*—the large landed estates concentrated in the island's centre. This area is currently regarded by sociologists as "classical" Sicily, and it is the one they most often observe and study, typically from the vantage point of the train route running from Catania, through Caltanissetta, to Palermo.

In this region, the owners of large estates rarely live in the municipalities where their lands are located. Instead, they prefer to reside in Palermo or another city on the island—and often in Naples, Rome, or even Paris. Nonetheless, there are a number of wealthy families—mostly newly enriched by the high rents from their land, which they sometimes still manage directly—who have not abandoned their ancestral homes. However, they are not numerous enough to form a true class: in a large rural municipality of twelve or fifteen thousand residents, there may be only one or two such families, and sometimes none at all.

Some of these families have recently acquired a notable degree of education, which, often combined with refined taste and genuine elegance of manner, allows them to exert a truly beneficial influence within their social sphere. Others, however, retain their former ignorance and inherited rustic coarseness, softened only slightly by a superficial veneer of gentlemanly behaviour. This behaviour typically reveals a distinctive mix of ostentatious courtesy and childish arrogance—an attitude that tends to particularly irritate Italians from the north.

Among the few wealthy families who still reside in the island's interior, some remain entirely detached from political and administrative life—whether out of distrust in public affairs, a preference for a quiet life, or even sheer selfish indifference. Those who do involve themselves do so with mixed results—sometimes doing great good, sometimes considerable harm—depending on the character and upbringing of those leading them.

When they cause harm, rather than working to preserve harmony between the *galantuomini* and the peasants—or even within the class of gentlemen itself—they become leaders of one of the factions into which the civil class of nearly every municipality is typically divided. In doing so, they often become the tools of the worst elements, who exploit their naïve arrogance and take advantage of their influence and wealth.

III.

Aside from the few families already mentioned, the vast majority of *galantuomini* in the rural areas of the large estates are far from wealthy. Those who own modest properties that, with careful management, can yield an income of three or four thousand lire per year[11] are already considered relatively well-off. However, although nearly all of them have a house and a small plot of land in the sun, most earn considerably less than that amount. Many are compelled—just to maintain appearances and scrape together the two thousand lire per year needed to uphold the dignity of a family that is almost always large—to resort to various strategies, which I will discuss later.

Ultimately, the financial situation of the *galantuomini* class in the interior of Sicily is quite similar to that of the *particolari* of Piedmont—small landowners living in the region's hills. However, while the *particolari* typically reside in the countryside, in homes situated on their own land, dress like well-to-do peasants, and—despite sometimes hiring a labourer or two—do not hesitate to plough their own fields, the Sicilian gentleman views life very differently.

Usually descended from a peasant who, three or four generations earlier, managed—through sharp intelligence, relentless labour, strict saving, and at times even usury—to build a modest fortune, the Sicilian *galantuomo* devotes himself to a continuous, determined, and often desperate effort to maintain his clothing, his status, and all the appearances of a civilized man (a bourgeois who does not live

11 17,000–22,000 USD.

by manual labour). Despite the ongoing fragmentation of wealth caused by the high birth rate of the Sicilian population, he strives above all to ensure that his children attain a position at least equal to his own.

Unfortunately, the means to emerge successfully from this struggle are limited and often ineffective. Along the island's coast, changes in farming methods—through which citrus groves, vineyards, and vegetable gardens have replaced the old barren fields and arid pastures—have led, despite frequent crises (usually caused by falling commodity prices), to such an increase in income that it has, to some extent, offset the effects of property fragmentation. These new crops even made it possible, during prosperous periods with strong market prices, to purchase, subdivide, and agriculturally transform many ancient estates once held by absentee landlords.

In the island's interior, however, due to climatic conditions and the greater difficulty of marketing agricultural products, such large-scale crop transformations have almost never succeeded.

In the interior, therefore, the more enterprising individuals—if they possess some capital—strive to lease or sublease a portion of a large estate. Others, having earned a degree or diploma, turn to the liberal professions, which offer only modest earnings in rural communities. Finally, some aim to secure a small private-sector job or... a position in the local administration.

IV.

The dream of every rural gentleman's family is for one or more of their children to earn a degree, settle in a major city, and achieve professional distinction in law or medicine—or even rise to a high-ranking position in the state administration. Those who succeed in fulfilling this ideal, whether fully or partially, are considered accomplished and gain considerable prestige and influence among their fellow townspeople, who often seek to crown their success by electing them to Montecitorio (Parliament). Conversely, those who fail to obtain a degree—or who, despite earning one, are unable to compete with other professionals and return to their native community—are regarded as failures.

To win this difficult race, there is no effort the young or old will not make, no sacrifice they will not endure. The famous Americans who began with just a dollar in their pocket and, through hard work, ingenuity, and luck, became billionaires, certainly possess a talent for big business that successful young Sicilian professionals often lack. However, it is extremely difficult to surpass Sicilians in tenacity—in their relentless determination to live and work solely in pursuit of success.

Within the family, everyone—men and women, fathers, mothers, brothers, and sisters—endures any hardship to support the one who shows the most promise. In turn, once that individual secures a position, they almost always devote a significant portion of their resources to helping their siblings and in-laws advance as well.

But unfortunately, while many are called, few are chosen. Moreover, even those few who are the most gifted often end up permanently distancing themselves from their hometowns. If the frequent absenteeism of landowners impoverishes the region economically, the absence of its most educated individuals impoverishes it intellectually.

In addition, families invest all their savings in supporting their future professionals, since scholarships are virtually non-existent in Sicily. It is estimated that the cost from high school through university graduation amounts to no less than twelve thousand lire[12]—sometimes representing half the wealth of a rural gentleman.

Often, however, the means to continue one's studies run out prematurely, or repeated academic failures bring an end to a university career. In such cases, the capital invested is entirely lost, and the young man returns to his village idle and embittered, now accustomed to smoking cigarettes and engaging in political gossip. He inevitably becomes a regular at the local *casino di compagnia* (a kind of youth club), an aspirant for a municipal job, and a behind-the-scenes player in political and administrative elections.

V.

The *casini di compagnia*, which I recently saw vividly and fairly accurately described in the *Corriere*, were generally established just over half a century ago. This happened after the complete abolition of feudalism and the introduction of large estate leasing—that is, when the first families of wealthy or well-off farmers began sending their children to study. When those children returned, they came back with a superficial layer of intellectual education.

In itself, it is not surprising that people who share the same—or nearly the same—social status, but have a culture and manners somewhat different from those of the common people, would form a shared meeting place. This, practically speaking, occurs almost everywhere. However, in the concentrated yet isolated environment of large rural Sicilian towns—where everyone lives within the village, interacts almost daily, and families seldom leave their birthplace—the establishment of the *casino* created a sharp social divide. On one side were those who, at a certain point, had attained

12 67,000 USD.

a particular social standing and their descendants; on the other, the rest of the population.

This clear and rigid social divide undoubtedly sharpens natural class antagonisms, making them feel almost hereditary and traditional. To be fair, it is not particularly difficult for the son of a wealthy farmer—after studying in the city and achieving a reasonable degree of financial independence—to be admitted, if he so desires, to the *casino dei galantuomini* (the gentlemen's club). However, it is very likely that he will not be held in the same regard as the son of a founding member, even if that founding member's son has been reduced to working as a notary's clerk for thirty lire a month.[13]

I often hear it said—and it is still frequently written today—that feudal customs persist in Sicily and that, especially in the countryside, life continues in a medieval atmosphere. However, such statements are usually made without offering any clear meaning or definition.

If the point is that large estates dominate part of the island, that fact is not unique to Sicily; similar conditions exist in other parts of Italy, such as the lower Novarese and lower Lombardy. And if Sicilian *latifundia* are less intensively cultivated than those in the Po Valley, I believe this is mainly due to geological and climatic factors.

If the comments refer to low agricultural wages, I would note that, thanks to emigration, wages have risen even in many of the island's inland towns. Similar wage levels can also be found in many rural areas of northern Italy—and in any case, wages on the island, as elsewhere, are determined by the law of supply and demand.

Ultimately, setting aside the posturing and rhetoric of

13 170 USD.

certain petty noblemen and focusing on the facts, what most evokes the feudal era in Sicily is the previously mentioned hereditary nature of social conditions in the inland towns—a heredity that is more formal than real, but for that very reason, all the more irritating.

In any case, it would be quite inaccurate to regard the modern *galantuomini* of central Sicily as successors to the grandeur and arbitrary power of the ancient barons. Rather, they constitute a small bourgeoisie—perhaps too numerous and certainly lacking in sufficient means—which, after struggling in vain to find remunerative work, resigns itself to the idleness of the *casini di compagnia*.

If this small bourgeoisie—serving as the region's ruling class—fails to generate new wealth, there are many mitigating factors behind that failure. It therefore deserves only limited reproach, especially since the fault is of a kind that carries within itself its own form of punishment.

Parties

I.

The internal conflicts among the factions of the ruling class, which now plague most rural municipalities in Sicily, have certainly been fuelled by the current political climate and the system by which municipal and provincial authorities are chosen through popular elections. However, the seeds of these conflicts were sown much earlier, tracing back to the period when Sicily was governed under the absolute—and at times arbitrary—rule of the Bourbon bureaucracy.

Since the Spanish era, in the old small royal municipalities—which, like the cities, depended directly on the Crown and therefore had no feudal lords—there were often two or three families of the provincial nobility residing there. These families were frequently divided by longstanding rivalries and animosities, competing in every possible way for a kind of local supremacy.

In municipalities that had belonged to feudal lords, those lords had, by the mid-nineteenth century, moved their residences to Palermo or Messina. Over the course of several generations, prominent families began to rise among the former vassals. These families initially accumulated wealth by managing the lord's lands, later by leasing them or holding them under long-term arrangements such as emphyteusis, and often eventually purchased the land outright after the abolition of feudalism in 1812.

Among these new families, rivalries quickly emerged—often even more bitter than those among the older noble houses. These conflicts arose from disputes over the lease of a fief, the rejection of a marriage proposal, or, in the most tragic instances, following a murder. Hatreds born from such causes—whether trivial or grave—soon became entrenched and traditional, particularly because of the confined nature of the environment.

In such settings, friends and enemies were forced to cross paths daily under the watchful eyes of the small world they shared—a world that constantly observed and judged them. This created a climate in which it became natural, almost inevitable, for passionate and unsophisticated men to adopt a modest version of Julius Caesar's ambition: unable to dream of being first in Rome, they burned with desire to be leaders in their large villages.

The high Bourbon bureaucracy was well aware of these local rivalries and exploited them when it served its own purposes. If it found that a wealthy and cultured rural family leaned toward liberal ideas, it would assign municipal offices and grant a kind of moral authority to a rival family deemed more reliably loyal to the Bourbon regime.

Furthermore, the leading figures of this bureaucracy—intendants, senior magistrates, generals, and gendarmerie colonels—most of whom came from major cities and carried the arrogance often bred by proximity to supreme power under absolute regimes, generally looked down on the petty nobility and rural bourgeoisie. To their credit, however, they were almost always incorruptible and, when politics was not at play, genuinely strove to uphold the law.

In the small municipalities—then almost entirely isolated from the rest of civil society—the law was enforced either by local figures, who knew all too well how to distinguish friends from enemies, or by the lower-level bureaucracy. This bureaucracy was poorly paid and easily corrupted; even when it did not openly accept bribes, it was often swayed by invitations, flattery, or gifts.

Through such means, the *galantuomini* of that time—fewer in number and relatively wealthier than those of today—were sometimes able to commit abuses against the peasants or exact petty revenge on their rivals.

II.

In 1860, between the outbreak of the revolution against the Bourbons and the establishment of the new regime under unified Italy, there was a period of semi-anarchy during which many grievances were aired and numerous acts of vengeance were carried out. It was during this time that massacres of landowners by peasants occurred in several towns, as previously noted in connection with the events at Grammichele.

However, it is important to note that the peasants' violent rage was almost always incited and directed by a landowner who had old scores to settle with rivals. One of the most effective methods of incitement was convincing the actual perpetrators that the recent revolution had made any excess permissible—and that it guaranteed them impunity.

Once order was finally restored—though it remained fragile for quite some time—the electorate responsible for choosing deputies, provincial councillors, and municipal administrators consisted of *galantuomini*, *maestri* (as artisans and small-scale entrepreneurs with modest capital are called in Sicily), and *borghesi* (wealthier peasants). However, the *galantuomini*, by virtue of their greater wealth, higher level of education, and greater experience in managing public affairs, held an almost absolute dominance.

The first thing they realized at the time was that the Italian prefect—sent from Rome—was far more pliable and had significantly less authority than the former Bourbon intendant. They also understood that under the new regime, officials could no longer dismiss a mayor or replace a municipal administration at will, as had been possible under the previous government.

They soon discovered that prefects and magistrates were dependent on ministers, who were generally receptive to the recommendations of deputies—deputies who, over time, increasingly accepted the requests of their most influential voters.

Experience then taught them that the range of functions and interests managed by municipal administrations was steadily growing, and that gaining control over these administrations was the most effective way to exert dominance within the local community.

Finally—generally after 1876—they learned, this time with the officials themselves often serving as instructors, that there was always a way to reach an understanding with representatives of the central government. They came to understand that the oversight these officials were meant to exercise over the preparation of electoral rolls, municipal administrations, and charitable institutions could be either extremely strict or remarkably lax, depending on whether the major voters in a community opposed or supported the ministerial candidate.

Once these lessons were absorbed, dealings with government authorities were made easier by the fact that political factions were already traditionally organized. In many rural communities, a network of loyalties, interests, friendships, and family ties had formed around the leading families—so negotiating with just a few key figures was often enough to secure several hundred votes.

As a result of these arrangements, the regime that has dominated much of the island for the past thirty years took shape. Its flaws are many and serious, and the author of this text had already pointed them out as early as 1883. Yet precisely because these flaws are so significant, there is no need to exaggerate them, as is too often the case.

III.

I have often heard it said—even by Sicilians—that the law in the island does not exist or is never enforced. There is also a widespread belief that nearly all rural municipal administrations in Sicily are nothing more than tools for plunder and exploitation, used by the *galantuomini* to shift almost the entire burden of local taxes onto the peasants and to allow the victorious faction to impoverish its rivals. It is further commonly claimed that these municipalities are burdened with an excessive number of employees, and that all municipal positions are filled through blatant favouritism.

Some of these accusations, in my view, are well-founded—though perhaps an even larger portion are not. It is important to recognise that the true root of the problem lies less in self-interest and greed, and more in the partisan spirit and the lack of fairness that such passions produce. This unfairness not only leads to actual abuses but also to exaggerated perceptions of abuse and a public outcry that would not arise elsewhere.

As for the claim that the law is not enforced, I can affirm that, in general, the laws—especially those concerning taxation and the obligations of citizens toward the state—are enforced with the same authority in Sicilian municipalities as they are in those of Northern Italy. The same applies to the Civil Code, the Commercial Code, and other legal frameworks. There may be some exceptions in the application of the Code of Criminal Procedure, but the most significant violations—usually committed in a way that offends the spirit rather than the letter of the law—tend to occur in the enforcement of electoral laws (both political and municipal/provincial) and in the administration of laws relating to charitable institutions.

As for the much-discussed accusations of extortion, the fact is that even among the smaller Sicilian municipalities, there are those that are wisely and properly governed. These are particularly successful when the dominant party is made up of wealthy and astute individuals who are careful not to give their opponents any legitimate grounds for complaint.

I also believe that if one could accurately calculate what the ruling class in Sicilian rural municipalities spends from its own resources on electoral battles, compared to what it dishonestly gains from municipal administration, the expenses (the former) would exceed the profits (the latter).

Regarding the claims that municipal taxes are used as a tool of exploitation at the expense of the poorer classes, I must point out that these accusations are often based on statistical studies. However, I do not believe that raw statistical figures can offer sound grounds for judgment to anyone unfamiliar with the broader factual context.

For example, I once read an article in a magazine that expressed outrage over the fact that four-fifths of the revenue in a small Sicilian municipality came from consumption taxes, which fell on nine-tenths of basic necessities such as wine and flour—products that had not yet been exempted. This might appear scandalous, but only to those unaware that the municipality in question was both small and very poor, and that its population included barely two or three families who regularly purchased anything beyond wine and flour.

In reality, when wealth is scarce and its expression even

rarer, it is inevitable that taxes will fall primarily on the poor.

Perhaps a more justified accusation is the one concerning the overabundance of municipal jobs and the partisanship often involved in appointing those who hold them. Indeed, where strong passions arise, there are always individuals ready to exploit them, and the intensity of administrative conflicts gives rise to a class of electioneering professionals who come to expect rewards for their efforts.

However, it should also be noted that such abuses provoke more uproar in Sicily than elsewhere—both because each party brings an exceptionally refined sense of administrative morality when judging the actions of its opponents, and because for every satisfied aspirant, at least ten are left disappointed. Whether or not these disappointed individuals are more qualified than those selected, they inevitably cry scandal and spread their grievances far and wide.

IV.

All things considered, it seems to me that the greatest harm lies in political demoralization.

In the small rural towns of Sicily, life is monotonous, and under the current conditions of economic and intellectual disorder, people's passions—except in cases of exceptional moral character—tend to be confined to local rivalries. This passion often takes on a morbid intensity, to the point that it erodes any sense of fairness or legality. People will commit, with complete indifference and to the detriment of their rivals, the very same acts they had just moments before loudly condemned in their opponents.

This passion frequently turns into a sentiment that, if not unique to Sicilians, is certainly more common among them than elsewhere. So much so that it is captured in a specific dialect word—*u currivu*—which has no equivalent in standard Italian, nor, I believe, in any other language.

The term refers to something deeper and more intense than mere stubbornness: it denotes the obsessive desire to win at any cost, and above all, to avoid appearing less powerful or clever than one's opponent—even at the expense of one's own personal interests.

It takes little reflection to see that in a country plagued by such a sentiment, it is often the government itself that exploits and encourages it, becoming its blind and irresistible instrument. One can thus clearly understand the anti-educational influence that political authority often exerts in Sicily.

It is not without reason, then, that on the island—and perhaps throughout Southern Italy—representatives of executive power, unless they earn respect through their personal integrity, are opportunistically flattered by the less virtuous and regarded with suspicion, or even contempt, by the rest of the public. What is currently unfolding in Calabria is merely one expression of this enduring mindset.

That said, the remedies for the excessive fervour of local factions in Sicily are not hard to identify. Greater wealth and better education could certainly, in Sicily as elsewhere, offer more productive outlets for human energy and guide passions more constructively. But the most immediate, moderating, and effective solution would be for Italy's governments to abandon the disgraceful practice of exploiting the moral weaknesses of the southern population for the sake of securing parliamentary majorities.

Latifundia and Peasant-Farmers

I.

The recent publications by Villari, Maggiorino Ferraris, Nitti, Alessio, Arcoleo, and Monzilli have certainly helped familiarize *Corriere* readers with the Sicilian question—not to mention the article by Colaianni, which presents a wealth of factual data and thoughtful observations.

However, forming a clear and accurate understanding of an economic and social environment—as well as physical conditions—that differ from those we are used to is so challenging that it is by no means inappropriate to revisit the subject. And since many of Sicily's problems, particularly the poverty of the peasant class, are commonly attributed to the existence of *latifundia* (large estates), known locally as *feudi*, it is with this issue that I will begin my discussion.

II.

I have already noted in a previous article that large estates and major leases are also found in many parts of the Po Valley, particularly in Lower Lombardy. Indeed, although there is now a tendency to divide them, large farms reaching—or even exceeding—five thousand *pertiche milanesi* (about three hundred and thirty hectares) are not uncommon.

However, while Lombard *latifundia* typically include not only a tenant's house—if not an even larger and more comfortable residence for the owner—but also the homes of the farmers who work the land permanently, along with numerous other structures such as stables, dairies, and warehouses, a Sicilian *latifundium* generally has only one main building. This structure usually contains a few modest living quarters and some storage rooms. Only on better-managed estates do simple stone stables begin to appear.

Nor do the differences end there. The *latifundia* of northern Italy are almost always perfectly flat, with their surfaces levelled to allow for full or partial irrigation. To this end, they are typically crisscrossed by numerous canals, often lined with rows of willows, poplars, and oaks.

On a Sicilian estate, by contrast, one rarely sees even a small cluster of trees near its sole building. Abundant and perennial canals are virtually unknown in the island's interior. On a property of four or five hundred hectares, there may be only a small spring—barely sufficient to supply water for people and livestock. Moreover, the centre of the island is generally a highly undulating plateau, with frequent and often steep slopes that make rational irrigation difficult, and in some cases, entirely impossible.

And there is more. On the Piedmontese plain, annual rainfall averages around eighty centimetres, while in Lombardy it reaches about one hundred. In Sicily, rainfall measures approximately seventy-five centimetres on the northern coast, between seventy and fifty on the eastern coast, and less than fifty on the central plateau—precisely the region where most of the *latifundia* are located.

In northern Italy, the driest season is winter, while the rainiest months are typically April and May—though summer rains are not uncommon, often accompanied by hail. In Sicily, by contrast, the rainiest season is winter, when the water is less beneficial and is mostly lost as swollen streams carry it unproductively to the sea. Rains begin again in April, become eagerly awaited in May, and then almost completely vanish from June through September.

Given all this, even a modest amateur in agriculture can easily understand why, in Lombardy, it is possible to harvest three or four cuts of hay each year even on non-irrigated land, while in Sicily only one is possible, and large-scale cultivation of rice, corn, and beans is practically unfeasible.

The only cereals widely grown on the island are wheat—yielding an average of eight quintals per hectare—and barley, which is harvested earlier than wheat. The only legume cultivated on a large scale is the broad bean, harvested in May. Naturally, livestock is scarce, especially cattle, and irrigated meadows or marshy land are almost non-existent.

III.

The true director and manager of a Sicilian estate is typically the principal tenant-farmer, or *gabelloto,* who decides the rotation schedule of agricultural practices to be applied across different parts of the estate. One portion is always left as open pasture, while another is dedicated to grain cultivation, usually preceded by the sowing of broad beans—a plant known for its strong nitrogen-fixing properties. Wheat is then sown for one or two consecutive years, and the cycle generally ends with a barley crop.

Pastoralism, along with the associated cheese production, is managed directly by the *gabelloto*. Once the land has been ploughed—using oxen owned by the main tenant-farmer—and the cultivation cycle is ready to begin, the land, usually divided into plots of four or five hectares, is subleased to individual farmers for a period of three or four years.

Each of these farmers is required to own a mule or donkey, transport manure to the plot, perform all the necessary labour, and typically give half of the annual harvest to the *gabelloto*.

This is the well-known sharecropping system, based on subleasing, which has long been—and continues to be—the subject of widespread criticism. In fact, investigations conducted about ten years ago revealed that the portion of the harvest retained by the sharecropping farmer represents, on average, a value of three hundred and fifty lire[14] per agricultural year.

This amount is clearly insufficient to support a peasant family for an entire year—especially when one considers the cost of maintaining a draft animal and the heavy burden of usury, as the small subtenant is almost always forced to seek advances during the winter months.

When the tenant cultivates the land directly or sublets it in plots larger than four or five hectares, it becomes necessary to rely on day labourers. Their wages—now significantly increased thanks to emigration—average around twenty-five cents per day (1.30€). Naturally, during the harvest season, these wages more than double.

However, it is not so much the low wages that cause hardship for day labourers in municipalities dominated by large estates, but rather the scarcity of work, which nearly vanishes for long stretches of the year. The cultivation of wheat, barley, and beans requires only ninety to one hundred days of labour.

This is also the primary source of the small subtenant sharecropper's misery. While it cannot be said that three hundred and fifty lire in provisions is inadequate compensation in Italy for one hundred days of actual work, it is equally true that no labourer can live decently for an entire year

14 2000 USD.

on the income from only one hundred days of employment.

And in this fact—so far little noticed—lies, in my view, the main explanation for the tendency of peasants in the interior of Sicily to remain clustered in the main towns of large rural municipalities. Undoubtedly, if they were to move their homes to the vast *latifundia*, they would find no opportunity to work or earn a single cent for two-thirds of the year.

By staying in the towns, however, they can always manage to earn some small supplemental income through their own labour and that of their wives and children.

IV.

Fortunately, not all of Sicily is made up of *latifundia* cultivated in the manner I have just described. About a century and a half ago, a movement toward radical agrarian transformation began. This movement—similar in many ways to what occurred in Puglia—has greatly intensified over the past forty years, aiming to replace grain cultivation and livestock farming with crops primarily intended for export.

As a result, especially in recent decades, the cultivation of citrus fruits and vegetables has expanded significantly in the smaller plains of Sicily where irrigation is possible, either through the diversion of springs or the digging of deep and costly wells. On the hills, mountain slopes, and plateaus, plantations of vines, olive trees, almond trees, carob trees, and nearly all arboreal plants suited to warm temperate climates have multiplied. Thanks to their deep root systems, these crops can survive the long summer droughts without the need for irrigation.

This transformation has brought—and continues to bring—several benefits. Foremost among them is the increase in the land's gross yield and, as a result, the overall wealth of the region. For example, one hectare of vineyard—currently among the least profitable arboreal crops—still generates about 500 lire (2,500€) worth of produce per year, whereas one hectare of wheat, rotated with pasture and beans, yields on average only 150 to 200 lire.

The second major benefit is the significantly greater demand for labour. Whereas previously only one agricultural worker was needed for about 100 days per year, after the transformation, at least two or three workers are required—and for a much longer period.

A third advantage is the close relationship in Sicily between agrarian transformation and the subdivision of land ownership. I observed this connection as early as 1894. Later, Einaudi demonstrated that a similar pattern exists in Piedmont, where the large estates of the lower Vercelli and lower Novara regions are consistently associated with cereal farming, while the cultivation of vines and mulberry trees is closely linked to the dominance of medium and small landholdings in the Asti and Monferrato areas.

Without dwelling on the necessity of this relationship—which can now be considered the result of a genuine economic law—I will simply state that it is an undeniable fact: throughout Sicily, wherever cereal farming continues, large estates not only persist but have even been reconstituted after previously being divided under special laws. In contrast, in areas where arboreal crops predominate, large estates naturally and almost inevitably become rare, while medium and small properties steadily increase.

At this point, readers from northern Italy may wonder why the entire island has not been transformed into a garden, a vineyard, or a plantation of fruit trees. Some might even assume that the lack of capital, the absenteeism, or the inactivity of landowners has prevented the widespread adoption of such a beneficial transformation.

I'll respond at once that while the causes just mentioned—such as lack of capital, absenteeism, and landowner inactivity—have certainly played a role, their impact has been minimal. A far more significant obstacle has been the various diseases that have afflicted the island's arboreal crops: citrus gum disease, the olive fruit fly, and above all, phylloxera, which alone has likely cost Sicily more than half a billion lire.

An even more serious—indeed, the principal—obstacle is the difficulty of selling the products of intensive agriculture at a profitable price. The low market value of these goods means that as soon as agrarian transformation extends beyond the humid and fertile coastal areas into the drier, colder central plateau—where transportation is also more costly and challenging—it ceases to be profitable.

V.

From this, it becomes clear that the solution to Sicily's agricultural problem—which closely resembles that of several regions in mainland Southern Italy—can only be achieved through two parallel and simultaneous strategies.

The first path is the one that has so far been adopted spontaneously: gradually replacing grain cultivation and pastoralism with tree crops. In this effort, the State can contribute only indirectly—by facilitating the marketing of Southern Italy's agricultural products both in the north and abroad, primarily through reduced railway tariffs and favourable trade agreements.

This leads to the need to pursue a second path, one on which only hesitant steps have been taken so far. This approach involves intensifying cultivation within the *latifundia* themselves—not by converting them to vineyards or orchards, nor by abandoning grain cultivation and pastoralism, but by improving these traditional practices and introducing new crops alongside them.

At this point, the problem becomes too technical to address fully in a newspaper article, so I will limit myself to mentioning two proposals that, in my opinion, deserve serious attention from experts.

Over the past decade, large-scale almond cultivation has been introduced on many large Sicilian estates with promising results. Rows of almond trees now break the monotonous barrenness of Sicilian fields and meadows. I believe a similar approach could be applied to mulberry trees, allowing for the development of silkworm farming—a practice that could bring the island several tens of millions in annual income, both through the rearing process and through the operation of silk mills. These mills would provide well-paid work for farmers, particularly women.

It should also be remembered that while the intensification of cereal cultivation and the creation of irrigated meadows in water-rich regions like Lombardy have relied on channelling natural water sources, in arid regions subject to long droughts, progress has been made through the construction of large reservoirs. These collect rain during the wet months and store it for irrigation during the dry season. Colossal works of this kind have recently been undertaken by the British in India and were historically carried out by the Moors in Spain—where some reservoirs still function effectively today.

If this method were adopted to irrigate even a modest portion of Sicily's large estates—supporting the development of irrigated meadows and the cultivation of maize and cotton—I believe a significant part of the island's agricultural problem would be resolved.

I should also mention the need for partial reforestation. However, this is a well-known issue on which experts are unanimously agreed.

I will therefore conclude this article—already longer

than intended—by expressing the hope that it may help readers in northern and central Italy understand that Sicilian *latifundia* are not left uncultivated, but rather are cultivated extensively. And given current conditions, extensive cultivation is likely the most rational approach available.

It is also to be hoped that scholars and sociologists now recognize that intensifying this form of agriculture is a highly complex and difficult challenge, as the honourable Colaianni has already rightly observed.

And given these characteristics, the problem cannot be solved by a law such as the one proposed in 1894 by the Honourable Crispi, which required landowners to grant so-called uncultivated lands in emphyteusis; nor by the proposal of the Honourable Sonnino,[15] which aimed not only to exempt small plots from taxation but also to reward absentee large landowners with half the land tax; and even less by the recent proposal of the Honourable Alessio, who suggested sending peasants from northern Italy to colonize a region already overpopulated, where emigration is often more of a blessing than a burden.

Rather, the problem can only be addressed through a coordinated series of measures, to be adopted gradually—once all Italians have a clear understanding of the conditions and needs of southern agriculture, and once the initiative of southerners themselves is better guided by a precise awareness of the realities of the global market.

15 Sidney Sonnino (1847-1922) a future foreign minister of the Kingdom of Italy and, together with prime minister Salandra, architect of Italy's entry into the first world war.

Why Has the Belief in State-Sponsored Poisoning Not Disappeared?

The echoes of the atrocious events in Verbicaro[16] have not yet faded, and new uprisings—sparked by measures imposed by authorities to combat the cholera epidemic and by widespread belief in its artificial origins—have erupted in Massafra, Sant'Angelo in Grotte, Cetara, and several other rural municipalities in southern Italy.

Certainly, in Verbicaro, a number of factors coincided to explain the uniquely tragic outcome. The municipality was not yet connected to the railway by a proper carriage road, hygiene conditions were neglected, and the local doctor lacked the trust and affection of the people. Moreover, the mayor struggled to maintain composure, as the outbreak of the epidemic revived painful and traumatic family memories.

However, these factors alone do not explain everything. The exceptional nature of the case was due not only to these specific circumstances but also to a particular psychologi-

16 In August 1911, following a cholera epidemic that affected much of the population, Verbicaro—a small town in Calabria—became the site of a popular uprising during which the mayor and the municipal secretary were killed, and the town hall was set on fire.

cal state among the population. This mindset led many to strongly suspect that the recent census had been conducted so that higher authorities could assess the surplus population, and that the epidemic had been unleashed because local officials had been ordered to eliminate that perceived excess.

This state of mind cannot be considered exceptional. While it does not extend across all of southern Italy, in many areas that once formed part of the former Kingdom of the Two Sicilies, numerous mayors—well aware of their constituents' attitudes—anticipated the dangers of conducting a census at a time when the epidemic was already looming in nearby towns.

In many rural municipalities of southern Italy, during a serious epidemic, the mayor, the local doctor, the magistrate, the police delegate, and the carabinieri officer—all local representatives of the State—might not be killed, partly due to fear of the consequences, such as imprisonment. However, they would almost certainly be suspected of deliberately spreading the disease and could easily be threatened—openly or anonymously—with a grim fate unless they ceased their alleged actions.

Thus, more than half a century after national unification, as the *Corriere* has already astutely noted, a deeply rooted mindset still persists among a significant portion of the southern population. This mindset reflects a particular worldview in which the entire bureaucratic and electoral structure—referred to broadly as "the State"—is seen through a dark and primitive lens: as a constant conspiracy by the powerful against the people, a fearsome instrument of oppression, and at times, even of death.

This is not the place to explore how such a collective mindset developed over the centuries—a mindset that has enabled, and continues to enable, such a grim vision to persist, even though it is largely imaginary, including in relation to the Bourbon era. Delving into this would confront us with one of the most complex problems in history, and since we prefer to avoid the overly simplistic explanations often put forward, it is best, for now, to set the matter aside.

This is not the place to examine how such a collective mindset developed over the centuries—a mindset that has made, and continues to make, such a grim vision possible, even though it is largely imaginary, including in reference to the Bourbon era. Exploring this would confront us with one of the most difficult problems in history, and since we prefer to avoid the oversimplified explanations so often put forward, it is better, for now, to set the matter aside.

What is of more immediate concern is understanding how and why fifty years of effort have done so little to change the aforementioned mindset.

Perhaps such an investigation will go a long way in dispelling many of the illusions held by the generation that came before us, and perhaps it will also postpone the fulfilment of some of our own hopes to the generation that follows. This would be a bitter but necessary realisation—especially if it prevents new illusions from taking root and offers us a clearer, more accurate understanding of the difficult problem we face.

When I was a young man, I often heard discussions about what is now called the Southern Question. Even then, Southerners of high intellect and spirit acknowledged that it was, as Senator Faina recently wrote, above all a moral issue—or, more accurately in my view, a psychological one.

Our well-meaning elders, who had fought for national unification, believed that once the Bourbons were removed, the mindset of the Southern masses would undergo a profound transformation within one or, at most, two generations.

The tools expected to bring about this rapid change included compulsory military service, improved transportation infrastructure, rising prosperity, and above all, the spread of education—viewed as a battle against ignorance, which was considered the root of all ills.

Military service once had a certain educational value, especially when long enlistments succeeded in instilling habits of character that differed from those of the environment in which a person was born. I remember, in fact, that thirty or forty years ago it was easy to distinguish—by demeanour, by way of speaking, or better, by reasoning—a southern peasant who had spent five years as a soldier from one who had never served under the flag.

Today, that distinction is almost impossible. Eighteen months or two years are not enough to transform the worldview of a labourer or alter his traditional ideas—perhaps also because such short service means that military education has become almost entirely technical. Undoubtedly, even now, the southern peasant is generally a good soldier, but as soon as he returns from the regiment, he shaves off his budding moustache and lets his sideburns grow. This rapid change in his face is a symbol of his prompt and complete return to the intellectual and moral habits of his home and native village.

The means of communication have multiplied, but they remain insufficient because railways and main roads are still not supported and extended by a dense network of secondary intercommunal and local roads. Transport difficulties, however, affect goods more than people, since the peasant does not yet aspire to educational or leisure travel. At most, he attends a festival or fair in a neighbouring village, or occasionally takes a short trip to the nearest city.

When he does travel today, it is usually due to transoceanic emigration. Yet throughout the journey and his stay in

America, he lives—so far as possible—among peasants from his own village or at least from the same province, in a state of near-total moral isolation. If he emigrates very young and learns English well, he often breaks this isolation and ends up settling permanently in America. But if he remains attached to ancestral customs and traditions, he almost always returns to his homeland with little more than a small sum of money—which, however modest, is still far greater than the number of new ideas he brings back.

The economic conditions of the southern agrarian populations have improved significantly, but this progress has occurred only in the past decade and is largely the result of emigration, which has raised wages and led to the accumulation of considerable savings in rural areas of the South. However, in every country, the first thing the lower classes do with an improved standard of living is to better their material circumstances. It is therefore not surprising that, for now, southern peasants eat better, dress better, and in some cases even live in better housing—but still feel no real need for newspapers, let alone magazines, lectures, or books.

That said, they have begun to send their children to school willingly, which is already a notable development.

All that remains to be addressed is education itself, which was meant to be the primary tool for dispelling ignorance, overcoming prejudice, and redeeming the southern populace both intellectually and morally.

Education—specifically elementary education, when it comes to peasants—spread only slowly until recent times, as shown by the statistics from 1902. This slow and limited progress was partly due to the lack of resources in rural municipalities, but the main reason was the passive resistance of the majority of those involved. While just a few years after 1860, artisans, shopkeepers, and small tenants—known in Sicily as *borghesi*—began to see the value in having their children learn to read and write, labourers and very small landowners—who made up three-quarters of the rural population in southern Italy—still saw no use in learning even basic arithmetic or the alphabet. It is well known that peasants everywhere are unwilling to make even the smallest sacrifice for something they see as useless.

Now, thanks especially to emigration, the southern populace has largely changed its outlook—perhaps because greater prosperity awakens new needs. In a few decades, this new attitude is likely to prove far more effective than all the other measures tried so far.

But one must not harbour any illusions: simply knowing how to read and write does not fundamentally change how a person—or even less so, a community—thinks and feels. Many of those who today believe that the mayor, acting on government orders, is spreading poison are perfectly literate. The many anonymous threatening letters recently sent to mayors across the South are proof of this.

Perhaps in fifty years, when it is hoped that all peasants will be free from illiteracy, they will no longer believe that a mayor could receive and carry out such a horrific mandate. But this change will not result from literacy and schooling alone—it will come because their mindset will have gradually evolved.

Indeed, even if by some miracle all living peasants were to wake up tomorrow holding an elementary school diploma, they would still hold the same beliefs they do today—on every subject, including infectious diseases.

I can already hear the objections from those who believe it will be easy to eliminate such a grim prejudice once the living voice of the teacher addresses it, and once newspapers and popular pamphlets explaining the basic principles of hygiene and the true causes of epidemics become more widely available. Unfortunately, these objections rest on another kind of prejudice—this time held by the educated—who assume that combating what they call ignorance is a simple task.

If the issue were simply one of ignorance, I would fully agree. But the real problem is that we are dealing with a kind of "false knowledge," and unfortunately, unlearning is far more difficult than learning. If the southern peasant knew nothing about the causes of an epidemic, it would be easy to teach them the truth. The difficulty lies in the fact that they already "know" a great deal about it—or at least believe they do, which, in practice, amounts to the same thing.

What they "know" is structured in their mind, linked to many other beliefs and traditions, and widely shared by other peasants—those they understand best and trust most. To make them abandon these beliefs, one would have to completely reshape their worldview and renew all their standards of judgment.

"We should all despair!" someone might exclaim at this point. Not at all—on the contrary, we have every reason to hope. Improved transportation, rising prosperity, the wider reach of elementary education, and, above all, the gradual spread of the educated mindset into the most humble layers of society have already had an impact—within certain limits—and will continue to do so with increasing force in the future.

If today the belief in State poisoning appears, in some cases, stronger than it did in 1866–67 or 1884–85, this is certainly not because it is more deeply rooted or more widespread, but rather because peasants now fear the authorities much less and therefore feel freer to express it openly.

One must acknowledge, however, that the means mentioned above act very slowly on the psychology of the masses. As Le Bon—one of the few serious writers in the social sciences—notes, this psychology has been shaped over centuries, and it will take centuries to dismantle it and complete the work of intellectual and moral assimilation that has only just begun.

Above all, to avoid delays and setbacks in this work of civilisation, it is essential not to repeat the mistakes of the past—or commit new ones that now risk overshadowing the near future.

For a long time, I asked myself whether it was more patriotic to remain silent or to speak out on certain issues. After much reflection, I have come to believe that the greater duty is to speak. I will therefore address the effects that universal suffrage may have in shaping the psychology of the southern populace, particularly with regard to beliefs about the artificial origin of certain infectious and contagious diseases.

What follows may come as a surprise to readers unfamiliar with the realities of the Mezzogiorno.

The conditions in Verbicaro and Grisolia, vividly described by Barzini, are truly exceptional, as it appears that in those towns the number of people entirely free from the belief in State poisoning is reduced to just a handful.

In most rural municipalities of the South, however, the vast majority of political and administrative voters no longer hold this belief—not so much because they can read and write, but because they are no longer peasant-farmers.

If, however, universal suffrage were introduced tomorrow in districts where the overwhelming majority are illiterate—and given that nearly all illiterates still believe the authorities spread poison—I would argue that the likely, if not inevitable, outcome would be the election of representatives who share that same prejudice.

But that would be a sensational claim—or rather, a falsehood. The truth is that, with very few exceptions, individuals free from this vile prejudice would still be elected. However, among them, preference would go to those who had the prudence not to oppose it too openly.

More precisely, I would add that, all other factors being equal, the greatest chance of success would certainly belong to those candidates who, with a vague remark or even just a knowing wink in response to a suggestive question, signalled that if elected to Montecitorio, they would know how to spare the constituency from outbreaks of acute gastroenteritis—and from all the burdens such epidemics impose on the poor: disinfection procedures, quarantine hospitals, and mayoral orders banning pigs from roaming the streets.

Thus, the educational work carried out—sometimes even unintentionally—by the more or less educated class of the South through its ongoing contact with the uneducated masses would largely be undermined and destroyed by the usual opportunism of political life. The slow process of assimilation, by which the best elements of the governed classes gradually adopt the mentality of the ruling class, would in part be reversed into a process where the worst elements of the ruling class adapt to and embrace the most odious prejudices of the governed classes. Unfortunately, this embrace would not be the only one, and as harmful as it is, it might not even be the most damaging.

And so, ultimately, among those northerners who boast that universal suffrage is the infallible remedy for the South's problems, there would be much talk—often quiet, perhaps more quiet than loud—about the South's incurable moral inferiority. Meanwhile, the poor South would once again fall victim to the doctrinaire political dilettantism of the Jacobin mania, which attempts to change people rapidly through decrees and laws, forgetting that such measures can only be effective when they align with the real conditions of society.

The Nasi Phenomenon Judged by a Sicilian

Nunzio Nasi[17] was convicted of embezzlement by the High Court of Justice, and just a few months after his sentence was pronounced, he was triumphantly welcomed back in his hometown. In various parts of Sicily—and even in some areas of mainland southern Italy—there arose, if not unanimous, at least a significant current of sympathy in his favour.

This very event, with its stark intensity, provokes comments and murmurs among honest people throughout central and northern Italy. It also astonishes foreigners, who, generally knowing little about our affairs—and even less about those of Sicily—wonder whether an entire city has gone mad, or whether crimes committed by certain individuals, under certain circumstances, are still regarded in some

17 Nunzio Nasi (1850–1935), born in Sicily, was a philosophy lecturer, a deputy in the lower house of parliament, and served as a minister on multiple occasions. In 1904, Nasi was accused of embezzlement related to his ministerial duties, found guilty, and forced to flee into exile in France and England. Nevertheless, his voters—believing him unjustly persecuted—continued to elect him to the Chamber of Deputies for the Trapani constituency. He successfully re-entered parliament in 1913 and, later in life, aligned himself with the antifascist opposition against the Mussolini government.

provinces of Italy as merits worthy of admiration.

Yet I can attest—and so can all those who have lived on the island for a long time—that Sicilians despise those who commit the crimes for which Nasi was convicted. If they still admire and celebrate the former deputy from Trapani, it is because the great majority of them, with perfect good faith, believe him innocent and are convinced that he was condemned simply because he was Sicilian.

Indeed, many on the island believe that, had a former minister from northern Italy been in Nasi's place, he would never even have been indicted. They think his conviction was primarily motivated by his extraordinary intellect and exceptional political talents, which would have inevitably led him to become Prime Minister—a path that personal rivalries, supported and fuelled by regional prejudices, sought to block at all costs.

It will likely be argued immediately that this explanation is even more improbable than the fact itself, and that it might provoke greater astonishment and surprise than the very apotheosis currently being made of the honourable Nasi. My interlocutors—often well-versed in Italian political affairs, to whom I have had to explain this issue several times—readily object that, in the current political generation, Sicily has produced dozens of individuals in the Chamber of Deputies and the Senate who far surpassed Nasi. They mention names such as Crispi, Rudinì, Gallo, San Giuliano, Maiorana, Orlando, Colajanni, and Pantano, noting how their Sicilian origins did not prevent their merits from being universally recognized throughout Italy.

However, the astonishment will fade, and the surprise will dissipate once we briefly clarify how and why the legend of Nasi was formed, by analysing the various factors that contributed to its creation: the character of the man, the unique environment of Trapani, and the nature of the

Italian political world.

In 1886, while the list-based voting system was still in use, the constituency of Trapani elected Nunzio Nasi as one of its representatives. The previous deputy was not a local and could be described as a conservative. In contrast, the new deputy was a young man from Trapani, a professor at the technical institute, reportedly an orator in the Masonic Lodge, and supported by the democratic faction. This political group consisted of bourgeois families who were either not very wealthy or had only recently acquired affluence. These families had not yet managed to integrate with the older, more established, and wealthier bourgeoisie and aspired to surpass them in influence within the local municipality, the province, and charitable institutions.

Naturally, the opponents of the new deputy assured others that he would make a poor impression in the Chamber of Deputies, while his supporters insisted he would have a brilliant political future. Some even claimed—though perhaps not entirely convinced—that within a few years he would become a minister.

In the early years of his political career, Nasi positioned himself as a moderate member of the extreme left, neither hostile nor overly deferential to Crispi. He liked to call himself a "savage" and maintained a somewhat independent stance. Later, during the first Cabinet led by Giolitti, he openly supported the government and joined the group of radicals who, because of their constant backing of the administration, were nicknamed the "squad of recruit carabinieri." Under Rudinì, he almost always voted with the opposition, although he maintained good personal relations with the marquis (Rudinì, the prime minister), and his criticisms of the government were always measured.

He spoke rather infrequently, but when he did, his speeches showed careful preparation, and occasionally he displayed moments of effective oratory. He lived simply, was withdrawn, and never practiced law—which, in any case, he had not pursued diligently before entering the Chamber. After a decade in Parliament, he had earned a reputation for integrity in his private life and consistency in his political actions. He had become a minor parliamentary figure and, because of his seniority, could be considered a potential minister.

And here I must allow myself a brief aside. If Nunzio Nasi were today what one might call a "liquidated" man, it would be unnecessary and even cruel to judge him publicly. But since he remains a prominent figure and the newspapers constantly report on his actions—his name becoming a symbol of internal unrest and external discredit—discretion regarding his reputation is no longer required or honest. What he is owed now is nothing but the truth, presented with the temperance that comes naturally when no hostile passion influences the writer.

In Italy, being considered "*ministeriabile*" (fit for a ministerial position) does not mean that a deputy is a person of exceptional intellectual and moral calibre, someone who has deeply reflected on domestic political issues and brings original ideas to the table. What is not superfluous is certainly not necessary, as shown by the fact that there are dozens of "*ministeriabili*" in the Italian Chamber of Deputies.

We all know that in every ministry, alongside some true talents, there are always individuals who—while not complete nonentities and capable of delivering a decent speech—can only claim an education and preparation no greater than what corresponds to the profession they held before entering politics. Such individuals owe their position to a set of causes often called "parliamentary combinations." These include belonging to a particular group and region, and being free from the intense antipathies within the

Chamber that often hinder the rise of more outstanding personalities.

Nasi owed his entry into the Cabinet formed in 1898 by Pelloux as Minister of Posts and Telegraphs to one of these parliamentary combinations.

However, it must be admitted that even as a minister, he was a "savage" in the political sense the Germans attribute to that word, making him difficult to classify.

He cannot be counted among ministers distinguished by intellectual stature or organizational skills, but neither does he belong to the secondary, colourless figures who merely fill out the Cabinets of the Kingdom of Italy.

The truth is that he undoubtedly owes all his fame to politics, which ultimately led to his downfall. Had he not entered Parliament at the age of 32, he would probably now be the headmaster of the technical institute, the respected master of the Masonic Lodge, and a councillor in the municipality of Trapani. However, his notoriety would not have extended beyond his province, and very few people—even in Palermo, let alone Rome—would have known of his existence.

Politics elevated him to great heights because it gave him the opportunity to develop two qualities that are eminently Sicilian, characteristic of the region where he was born, and which he possesses to the highest degree: an unbounded confidence in himself and his destiny, and an indomitable tenacity. This tenacity ensures that a man never considers himself definitively defeated in the grand contest he wages with the world for success, and it drives him to persist in his struggle not only when teetering on the edge of the abyss but even after having fallen into it.

Moreover, Nasi, who during the three years he served as Minister of Public Education did not initiate the reorganization of his department but rather increased its confusion, and who never expressed any truly profound or original ideas about Italy's present or future, developed only two concepts during the long years he spent as a deputy and minister. These—perhaps already sketched out in Trapani—dominated his thinking and guided his actions as a minister: namely, that the fame of politicians is created and sustained by newspapers, and that to remain in power, it is necessary to grant many favours to friends and inspire great fear in adversaries.

The qualities mentioned above and the methods described can be very useful in politics—provided the former are supported by other virtues and the latter are applied with tact and moderation. However, moderation, tact, and a few other necessary qualities were lacking in Minister Nasi, especially during his time at the Ministry of Public Education.

In fact, he who so loved newspaper praise and did so much to obtain it became the first victim of his own game, placing great importance on that praise. He took it seriously because his confidence, having soared to such heights, turned into a dogma of his own superiority and a blind belief in his infallibility. Consequently, he viewed laws and regulations as mere obstacles to his reforming genius, saw all opposition and criticism as motivated by envy, and believed himself entitled to many—too many—privileges that he would have severely punished in others.

He granted favours to all who asked—politicians, individual professors, employees, and his own voters—regardless of the moral character of these requests. Yet there were also those who did not ask for favours, and others who, after receiving them, failed to repay him with unwavering loyalty or unconditional admiration.

It was at this point that something resembling a persecution complex emerged—or rather, developed—in him. This was not madness, but it robbed him of the ability to perceive and assess objectively the reasons behind others' behaviour toward him. It was a kind of intellectual squint, so to speak, found to some degree in all those who think too highly of themselves and lack self-criticism.

As a result, he became suspicious of everyone and ended up offending many, harming others, alienating friends, turning neutral parties into adversaries, and transforming many of those into enemies.

And now, back to Trapani. Trapani is not a large city, but it is industrious and hardworking, and naturally not indifferent to the allure of worldly and political glory. It was the charm of this glory—far more than a certain number of small personal favours—that bound the city to its deputy.

In Trapani, success transformed Nasi's former supporters into passionate admirers, and even among his old opponents, many competed zealously to acknowledge the greatness of their fellow citizen, trying to make amends for the delay in recognizing it.

For two or three years, Nasi was regarded throughout Italy as a man of elevated intellect, a hope for the democratic constitutional party, and it was considered possible that he might become Prime Minister. Many newspapers from Rome, Naples, and Milan praised the speeches he delivered as he toured the peninsula. Today, he would be applauded in Asti or Venice; tomorrow, his arrival in Milan or Turin would be considered an event.

It is true that discordant voices occasionally arose here and there, but first, they rarely reached Trapani, and second, they were easily dismissed as personal rivalries or partisan hatred. Ultimately, no one could deny that even the northerners—so proud of their superior culture—recognized Nasi as a first-rate political figure, and that everyone, including his opponents, acknowledged his talent.

Under these conditions, it is no surprise that the bourgeoisie of Trapani felt very proud and pleased that a future Prime Minister—who seemed destined to surpass the fame of Crispi—had emerged from their midst. Likewise, it is unsurprising that the common people of Trapani came to see their deputy as an extraordinary man, almost like a deity.

Naturally, around this idol, a priestly group formed, tasked with maintaining the cult. Among them were several ambitious individuals who, while waiting for Nasi to be called to the position of Prime Minister, were content to hold all the local offices in Trapani under his powerful protection.

When the storm arrived, admiration for Nasi had already become deeply rooted among the masses of Trapani, and the interests built around this admiration had grown too strong for either the masses or those interests to easily accept defeat.

It is worth noting, first of all, that Sicilians do not easily admit to being deceived and rarely abandon their friends or those to whom they have entrusted their loyalty during times of trial and adversity. Furthermore, nearly all the newspapers on the island—especially those read by the working classes—have always presented the most favourable narratives about Nasi.

Nevertheless, there were elements that made defending the thesis of Nasi's innocence not too difficult, at least within Sicily.

It is indeed true, as is often said, that Rudinì, Colajanni, Orlando, and Maiorana—against whom the so-called envy of the northerners has never been directed—have a personal stature far superior to that of Nasi. But how many in Sicily possess the ability and the necessary knowledge to make such a judgment? There, as elsewhere, the vast majority judge politicians based on what newspapers say about them, and these newspapers have perhaps focused more on Nasi than on all four of the figures I just mentioned.

Furthermore, there is no shortage of arguments containing so much truth that the small amount of error and malice concealed within them becomes almost imperceptible to a passionate mind.

It is undeniable, in fact, that other Ministers of Public Education committed irregularities, yet no one thought to bring them before the High Court of Justice. We know well that these were minor irregularities and that those responsible acted in ways that made it easier for them to be forgiven. But who will convince his fellow citizens that Nasi was not forgiven because he was from Trapani—or rather, because he was Sicilian?

Here a more complex, painful, and serious issue arises. For it will be asked: how can it be believable in Sicily that simply being Sicilian could attract enmity and resentment on the Italian mainland, and, in any case, that it could lead to harsher consequences and a less impartial judgment of a man's actions?

For now, I will answer simply—but with deep sadness—that this can happen because what the Germans call the "Weltanschauung" of the people—the collective psychology of the masses—is still quite different in northern Italy from that of Sicily. Between two such distinct collective psychologies, which find each other difficult to understand, misunderstandings are easily fostered.

Moreover, even in other countries there have been events closely resembling the condemnation and apotheosis of Nasi. In France, the differing psychology of two parties—two traditions—divided the country over the moral judgment of the sentence imposed on Dreyfus. There, as here, the objectively better cause—the one that should have triumphed because it could be more easily defended before impartial observers and foreigners—was embraced by the side with greater skill.

And now, let us conclude with some other melancholic reflections.

It is certain that, for the time being, the popular sympathies of Trapani—and, here and there, those of Sicily and the southern mainland of Italy—will continue to favour Nasi. Because if it is difficult to instil a concept and sentiment into the hearts and minds of the masses, it is even more difficult to uproot them swiftly.

But outside of Trapani, where Nasi will continue to be re-elected several times, these sympathies will be sterile. The ruling classes of Sicily have largely never supported Nasi, and if they have not openly opposed him—so as to avoid unpopularity—they have never truly endorsed him. Ultimately, perhaps no one knows the faults of the deputy from Trapani better than the deputies and senators from the rest of Sicily, and no one considers it less desirable than they do for him to return as a powerful and fear-inspiring figure.

An exception to the rule is the group from Trapani who now lead the demonstrations and who, while they still hoped for an acquittal from the High Court, counted on the future premiership of their fellow citizen. But probably, even among them, many must now confess to themselves—if not to others—that they were wrong and may be seeking a decent way to extricate themselves from their embarrassment.

Finally, scattered not only throughout Sicily and the South but across all of Italy, remains a large cohort of those who, in better times, proclaimed Nasi a great man, elevated him to a first-rate political figure, and asked for and received support and favours, even though they knew these were illicit. These individuals, by exploiting his flaws and ambitions, indirectly helped him create and benefit from the illusions of his fellow citizens and fellow Sicilians.

Today, most of those who belong to this category of former partisans and admirers of the ex-minister prefer to remain silent; or, if they live far from Sicily, they speak and write with pity and regret about the inhabitants of that generous island who, due to an incomprehensible distortion of moral sense, applaud a common criminal convicted of embezzlement by Italy's highest court, the High Court of Justice.

The Death of Antonio di Rudinì[18]

This evening, at 10:40 PM, the Marquis Rudinì passed away peacefully, without suffering in his final moments.

Around his bed stood all his relatives, some friends, and the honourable Maresca. The news of his death was immediately telegraphed to the King, the Queen Mother, the royal princes, and the Prime Minister.

By 2:30 PM, he had entered agony, according to a bulletin signed by the attending physicians, Maresca and Zeri.

The dying man appeared to have used his last reserves of energy during the dramatic events of the previous day, as after that he remained in almost continuous prostration.

I have already informed you about what happened yesterday when Monsignor Beccaria offered religious comfort to the ailing man. However, I must add that the Marquis of Rudinì was neither anti-religious nor atheist; on the contrary, he respected others' faith but was not himself a practitioner. Monsignor Beccaria, a longtime family friend, visited Villa Leonia daily and returned again last night, spending much of the night with the patient. He also came

18 Antonio Starrabba, Marquis of Rudinì, (1839–1908) was an Italian statesman from Palermo, and Prime Minister of Italy between 1891 and 1892 and from 1896 until 1898.

back today, staying the entire day and bringing holy oil to administer should the patient, in one of his lucid moments upon seeing the priest by his bedside, express the desire to receive it.

The ailing man lay motionless, stretched out with a waxen face that often showed spasmodic contractions. His laboured, drawn-out breathing and an anguished rattle were the only signs of life remaining.

The room was filled with a deathly silence, broken only by suppressed sobs.

At 6 PM, the Duke of Aosta arrived at Villa Leonia in a rented carriage. He was received by the Marchioness of Rudinì and her son, Deputy Carlo. On behalf of the King, the royal family, and himself, the prince expressed his deepest condolences. The Duke briefly saw the illustrious patient but chose not to disturb his final moments, though he remained in the Rudinì household for a long time. Deeply attached to the unfortunate marquis, the Duke left Villa Leonia visibly moved.

Since yesterday, following the announcement of the Honourable di Rudinì's worsening condition, a steady stream of people anxious for news has continued unabated at the villa on Via Quintino Sella. Hundreds of telegrams have arrived from all over. An aide-de-camp of the German Emperor sent a telegram on his behalf, as did nearly all the ambassadors and foreign representatives accredited to the kingdom.

The Honourable di Rudinì now lies in his small bed; his face is waxen but calm, like that of someone asleep. His hands rest on his chest, and two candles burn at the foot of the bed, where two nuns pray.

The news of his death began to spread after 11 PM, causing a profound impression despite being expected. Calls flooded Villa Leonia from everywhere, seeking confirmation of the sad news.

Among the final wishes expressed by the Honourable di Rudinì was his desire to be placed, after death, in a modest coffin wrapped in a white sheet.

The Man, the Statesman

The Marquis Antonio Starrabba di Rudinì was born in Palermo on April 6, 1839. The Starrabba family, of ancient provincial nobility, originated from Piazza Armerina—one of the many Sicilian towns founded by the Lombard and Monferrato colonies that settled on the island in the early 12th century. About two centuries ago, the Marquis's ancestors moved to Palermo, where they formed marital alliances with some of the most illustrious families of the Sicilian nobility.

In his early years, Rudinì was privately tutored before attending the law program at the University of Palermo. At that time, the Palermo university had few renowned professors, though Rudinì did have a few good ones, and he always cherished the memory of lessons taught by Bruno, an economist of some significance associated with the Bastiat school.

At Twenty

But 1859 arrived, marking the beginning of the political life of the future Prime Minister of the Kingdom of Italy. Rudinì, then twenty years old and an opponent of the Bourbons—like most of the Sicilian nobility and bourgeoisie—soon became convinced that only the Savoy monarchy could grant Italy both unity and independence, along with a genuinely constitutional regime. He therefore conspired and joined a revolutionary committee preparing the island's insurrection under the cry of "Italy and Vittorio Emanuele."

Much of the work of this committee underpinned the

premature revolutionary movement of April 4, 1860, which was brutally suppressed. The Bourbon authorities became aware of Rudinì's involvement in the plot, forcing him to flee to Naples. From there, skilfully evading police agents seeking to arrest him, he boarded a French ship and sailed to Genoa.

Having learned of the expedition that had departed from Quarto a few days earlier, Rudinì attempted to return to Sicily on the steamship Gulnara of the Sardinian merchant navy. However, when the Gulnara neared the island's shores, it was spotted by Neapolitan warships patrolling the area to prevent any landings of exiles and volunteers. As a result, the captain decided to return to Genoa. This is why Rudinì was not in Palermo on May 27th, the memorable day of Garibaldi's entry into the city.

As soon as the Kingdom of Italy was proclaimed, the young marquis was appointed attaché to the Ministry of Foreign Affairs, and in this role, he lived in Turin for several years. When he later became Minister of Foreign Affairs, he often liked to recall this period of his youth, during which he encoded and decoded many dispatches. He used to say that in this seemingly entirely mechanical task, he observed and learned many things. Perhaps he learned even more through conversations with the most illustrious men of Italy who gathered in the capital of the new Kingdom, many of whom he came to know personally.

His Actions in Palermo

Meanwhile, in Palermo, the moderate faction managing the municipal administration in the first decade after the revolution needed the contribution of its youngest and most dynamic members. The Bourbon regime had left the island's main city in truly deplorable conditions: few or no elementary schools; streets, except for a very few, were poorly paved and even more poorly lit; no effort was made to curb the common people's habit of occupying public spaces; and hygiene and urban sanitation services were almost non-existent. In short, almost everything had to be established or rebuilt from scratch.

Rudinì was therefore convinced that his efforts were far more necessary serving the Municipality of Palermo than the Ministry of Foreign Affairs. Once returned to his native city, he was appointed Mayor in 1864.

This was perhaps the period of his life when he had the greatest confidence in his own efforts and energy. The drive he provided was so significant that, in less than a decade, the city underwent a material transformation, and its municipal services—according to the testimony of many contemporaries—became comparable to those of the most advanced major Italian cities.

In 1877, when Gladstone asked Minghetti which Italian city had made the greatest progress after the overthrow of the old regimes, Minghetti replied without hesitation: Palermo.

Naturally, such radical and sudden changes were bound to clash with long-standing habits, harm many interests, and consequently generate significant discontent. Adding to the unrest in the city and throughout the island were several factors: the recent introduction of conscription; the increase of old taxes and the imposition of new ones; the confiscation of properties belonging to suppressed religious congregations—which left many families destitute and deprived others of donations and subsidies; and the incompetence of many government officials, who were generally unfamiliar with the local environment and some of whom barely concealed, or even flaunted, their disdain for all things Sicilian.

On top of this, in 1866 came the misfortune of an unsuccessful war[19] and the introduction of paper currency, which lost as much as fifty percent of its value in exchange. This was perhaps the only moment when Sicily truly had all the elements for a revolutionary movement—or at least a violent rebellion—that could rely on the support of a segment of the less educated and poorer classes.

The Heroic Moment

And indeed, the revolt broke out in Palermo on September 16, 1866. For several days, it had been known that several hundred draft evaders and bandits were roaming the mountains surrounding the city, ready to invade and rally the populace to arms. The garrison had been reduced to a few hundred grenadiers due to the demands of the war. On the evening of September 15, Rudinì and other prominent citizens—who had reliable information about the situation—went to Prefect Torelli and urged him to summon the National Guard that very evening so it would be ready to face the events at dawn the next day. The Prefect resolutely refused, though the reasons for his refusal remain unclear.

The next morning, at a very early hour, armed bands entered the city shouting, "Long live the Republic!" ("viva la Repubblica"). The young mayor, leading about fifty members of the National Guard and a platoon of grenadiers, immediately began patrolling the streets and sounded the general call to gather the city militia. However, the populace had already risen in revolt, intercepting communications, and the few National Guards who dared to venture out were easily surrounded and disarmed.

During the night, the small group gathered around the mayor managed to retreat to the Royal Palace, where the

19 The third war of Italian independence (against the Austrian Empire).

Prefect, other authorities, a few National Guards, and a handful of soldiers had also taken refuge. There, for another four days, they bravely resisted against many thousands of insurgents.

When, due to scarcity of food and ammunition, some began to suggest negotiations and surrender, Rudinì—this time supported by Torelli—indignantly rejected the idea of coming to terms with anarchic bands that represented no political ideology but merely rebellion for rebellion's sake.

Victory Over the Rebels

On the sixth day of the insurrection, an entire division of the regular army managed to disembark, establish communication with the Royal Palace, and seize control of the suburbs after several hours of combat, during which both sides suffered hundreds of casualties. The following day, at noon, the rest of the city was occupied by the troops with little resistance.

Throughout Italy, the young mayor's name—thanks chiefly to his efforts—was justly celebrated for preventing Palermo from falling completely under the control of an insurrection without a program or recognized leaders.

Almost immediately, in organising the health service to combat the cholera ravaging his city, Rudinì demonstrated further evidence of his calmness and his ability to select the most suitable men for delicate and difficult missions. A few months later, the government appointed him Prefect of Palermo. With his tact and energy, he greatly contributed to the complete restoration of internal order under the Menabrea Cabinet and to the eradication of brigandage throughout the province.

In 1868, he was appointed to oversee the Prefecture of Naples, where he demonstrated political awareness and the qualities of a capable administrator. He even had to thwart a Mazzinian (republican) conspiracy, arresting, among others, two young Sicilians. One of these would later become a Minister and, many years after, an influential member of the far-left; the other remains today a well-educated and resolute member of the republican faction. Both held no lasting grudge against him and, over time, became his personal friends.

The strong performance Rudinì demonstrated in all the positions he held greatly enhanced the authority of his name. So much so that, when Ferraris resigned as Minister of the Interior in September 1869, the thirty-year-old Marquis—still not a member of parliament—was called to replace him. However, after seventy days, the Menabrea Cabinet fell, and Rudinì immediately returned to the Chamber of Deputies as the representative of the Canicattì constituency.

The Parliamentary Beginning

And here began a new phase of his life, seemingly less active than the one that had unfolded in the previous decade. During this period, the young deputy—though far from power and public office, but not from politics—had the opportunity to deepen his knowledge and, through studies, travels, and continuous contact with the parliamentary world, to develop a clear and very secure understanding of people and affairs.

He faithfully served in the ranks of the old Right until March 18, 1876, when Depretis began his policy of "*trasformismo*." Rudinì considered Depretis' policies harmful to the political faction to which he had devoted all his youthful energy, because they forced it to abandon its banner and lose its distinct identity—an identity that could still attract new forces and offer fresh service to the country. When he was not listened to, he joined Silvio Spaventa and a few others to form a group of right-wing dissidents, which almost always voted against the various Ministries led by Depretis until 1887.

During that period, he often took an active role in parliamentary work and delivered notable speeches, praised for their balance, precision, and independence of thought. The Chamber showed its trust in him by electing him as its vice president in 1882, and he was re-elected to this position—with only a few brief interruptions—until 1891.

In 1887, when Crispi came to power amid the country's almost unanimous expectations, Rudinì abandoned systematic opposition but did not give unconditional support to the new government. At that time, he described himself as a political loner, and in truth, his beliefs and judgments about events did not align with those of his Right-wing friends, who mostly supported Crispi, nor with the far Left, which opposed him.

The mentality of the former mayor of Palermo differed too greatly from that of the new Prime Minister, and this kind of incompatibility in character occasionally surfaced in the Chamber. In fact, veteran deputies may recall a brief, bitter, and lively oratorical duel in which Crispi—using an unfair interpretation of events acknowledged even by his own Left-wing supporters—reproached Rudinì for having fought only during the disastrous days of September 1866.

The First Rudinì Ministry

Then came the elections of 1890, from which the Right emerged strengthened. However, discontent in the country grew due to the economic crisis that had been tormenting it for nearly three years, and the large deficit in the state budget could no longer be concealed. Under these conditions, another impulsive and unjust statement by Crispi triggered the crisis of January 31, 1891, leading to the arrival of the first Rudinì Ministry.

Here begins the third phase of Antonio Starrabba's political life, and at the same time, we fully enter contemporary history, with events clearly remembered by all who have reached the age of thirty. It is well known that the first Rudinì Ministry—which included Luzzatti, Chimirri, Nicotera, Villari, and Colombo—had the fundamental goal of restoring public finances, making them the cornerstone for the country's economic recovery. To achieve this, the ministry embarked on a period of strict economy and both internal and external consolidation, opposing any colonial expansion and even taking pride in the nickname "Ministry of the Thrift."

However, thrift never made a man or government popular, and Rudinì and the other ministers lacked a broad parliamentary base. Therefore, despite accepting support from part of the far-left, particularly the radicals led by Cavallotti, they were overthrown in May 1892.

The first Giolitti Ministry followed, and at the same time, the socialist faction in the country grew stronger, becoming a new and important factor in Italian politics. Later, the workers' leagues (*fasci dei lavoratori*) emerged in Sicily, the scandal of the Banca Romana[20] broke, and an investigation into the relationships between politicians and the banks ensued. This investigation brought down the Giolitti Ministry, tarnished the reputations of many politicians, but left Rudinì's reputation unscathed.

Perhaps if Rudinì had been called to power in November 1893, Italy would have been spared a great misfortune. However, at that time, many—including some in high places—believed that Crispi was better suited to handle the events.

Instead, one of the most turbulent and tragic periods in

20 The fall of Banca Romana in 1893 triggered the creation of the Bank of Italy.

Italy's contemporary history followed. In just over two years, there were the state of siege in Sicily and Lunigiana, the continuation of the banking scandal, the moral question, the victory at Coatit, the conquest of the Tigre, Amba-Alagi, and finally Abba Garima.[21]

African Politics

Rudinì, a consistent opponent of expansionist policies in Africa, was called upon to resolve the situation, and his second Ministry, which began on May 7, 1896, brought the African adventure to a close. While the resolution was not beyond criticism, it certainly reflected the wishes of a large portion of the Italian populace at the time.

It was far more challenging to restore calm within the country, rebuild trust in the government, heal the wounds of the prolonged economic crisis, and address the moral crisis by halting the process of disintegration that, from 1893 to that point, had been eroding the structure of the Italian state and society. Undoubtedly, Rudinì made mistakes in this extremely difficult task, but many were inevitable consequences of earlier errors made by others. There can be no doubt that the scandal of Banca Romana, the moral crisis, and Abba Garima were the three main factors behind the psychological state of the nation that led to the grave events of 1898.

Overwhelmed by these events, Rudinì fell from power and, for an entire decade, resisted the temptation of easy justifications. He never directly responded to those who, after attacking him in June 1898 for his perceived weakness and supposed collusion with the radicals, later reversed

21 The Italian military defeat in March 1896, at the decisive battle of the First Ethiopian War, halted Italy's colonial ambitions in the Horn of Africa for many years.

their stance, labelled him a fierce reactionary, and formed alliances with the socialists.

Nonetheless, he continued to attend the Chamber of Deputies regularly, though he rarely participated in its public debates. Noteworthy, however, were his vote and speech in February 1901, when he supported the faltering Saracco Ministry, and the loyal support he gave to the short-lived Sonnino cabinet of 1906. Those well-versed in parliamentary affairs can appreciate the nobility of the motivations that guided the Sicilian statesman's political actions on those occasions.

The Farmer

One of the few accolades rarely denied to Rudinì was that of being an excellent farmer. Indeed, he intelligently intensified the cultivation of his vast estates in Pachino, in the province of Syracuse. He replaced the traditional Sicilian latifundia practices of open grazing and grain cultivation with plantations of almonds, carob, and especially vineyards. After his vineyards were devastated by phylloxera shortly after 1890, he was among the first to rebuild them using American rootstocks.

His wineries, machinery, and all his agricultural facilities ranked among the finest in Sicily, and his expertise in enological matters was undisputed. The labourers who worked his lands were always fairly compensated, and there were never any strikes or grievances among them.

Opinions about Rudinì as a politician are, naturally, more varied. While the sincerity of his intentions has been widely acknowledged, he has long faced—and continues to face—accusations of limited ability, incomplete education, and lack of willpower.

The persistence of such claims has always puzzled most of those who had the honour of knowing Rudinì intimately.

They knew that his intelligence was evident, precise, and insightful; that his observational skills were keen and often profound; and that his memory was remarkably strong. While he might not have been truly extraordinary or what one might call a genius, he undoubtedly possessed a highly cultivated mind. They also recognized that his expertise in historical, economic, and social disciplines was such that few parliamentarians of his generation could match him.

Lastly, they were aware that once he made a decision—whether good or bad—he was determined to carry it out, subordinating everything to achieving the part of his program he considered fundamental. This was evident in his unwavering efforts to balance the budget during both his ministries and in securing peace in Africa at the start of his second. Furthermore, when circumstances demanded, he did not shy away from any responsibility, as he demonstrated on numerous occasions both before and after his time in government.

On the other hand, those who have not only personally known Rudinì but also studied the mentality and psychology of the masses can easily understand the reasons behind the limited enthusiasm he inspired. As a nobleman who reached prominent positions at a very young age, it is unsurprising that he was often seen not as a self-made man but rather as someone privileged by birth and favoured by fortune.

Few recognize that, without a certain degree of luck—regardless of whether one comes from the highest or lowest social strata—no one rises to prominence. While an elevated birth undeniably facilitates the initial steps in any career, in today's world it no longer suffices to compensate for shortcomings in character or intellect when occupying exalted and demanding roles, constantly exposed to relentless criticism from implacable adversaries.

It must also be acknowledged that our Sicilian gentleman, despite possessing some essential political qualities, lacked others. He understood enough to serve his country effectively; however, especially in his later years, he lacked the enthusiasm, fervour, and unwavering self-confidence that inspire trust in others. Always measured and proper, he failed to recognize that a politician performs on a stage, where gestures must be more exaggerated and words more resonant than in everyday life. As a result, his simplicity and natural demeanour often made him seem dull, which alienated applause.

The Man of Government

Naturally aristocratic in the best sense of the word, Rudinì never fully adapted to the demands of parliamentary life and was therefore never solely motivated by the desire to defeat his opponents or appease his allies. He did not shape every act or word to fit a program aimed solely at gaining or retaining power, nor was he lavish with favours or ruthless in his vendettas. As a result, he failed to build around himself the cohort of interested parties that, more than popular acclaim, perhaps best secures the position of a party leader or head of government.

In the political world, he was more respected than loved—if by love one means a bond rooted in gratitude or complicity—and, most significantly, he was hardly feared. His power, when he held office, rested more on the circumstances of the moment and temporary alliances than on a solid parliamentary base. His governments always had an air of precariousness and left an impression of weakness.

It is universally known that Rudinì was a man of simple, courteous, and dignified manners, and that he remained steadfast in his private friendships. While he never held an excessively high opinion of many widely celebrated parliamentary figures, neither did he have an inflated view of himself. In a rare quality for politicians, he was never guilty of vanity or presumption. Perhaps even rarer, he was able to recognize and appreciate merit, even when it was not accompanied by fame or an elevated social or political position.

History, when it studies the Marquis of Rudinì without prejudice or passion, will likely enhance his reputation by comparing him to many of his contemporaries. While it will acknowledge his errors, it will also recognize the good he did and, above all, the harm he managed to prevent.

Bibliographic Appendix

Primary Sources by Gaetano Mosca

Mosca, Gaetano. *What Is the Mafia?* 1901. Translated manuscript essay. Originally published in Italian as "Che cosa è la mafia?" in *Nuova Antologia*, vol. 177 (1901).

Mosca, Gaetano. *Men and Things of Sicily: Selected Essays.* Compiled and translated collection, early 20th century. Originally appeared in various issues of *Nuova Antologia* and other periodicals, 1890s–1900s.

Mosca, Gaetano. *The Ruling Class.* Translated by Hannah D. Kahn. New York: McGraw-Hill, 1939. Originally published as *Elementi di scienza politica*. Torino: Fratelli Bocca, 1896.

Secondary Sources on Gaetano Mosca and Political Sociology

Michels, Robert. *Political Parties: A Sociological Study of the Oligarchical Tendencies of Modern Democracy.* Translated by Eden and Cedar Paul. New York: Hearst's International Library Co., 1915. Originally published as *Zur Soziologie des Parteiwesens in der modernen Demokratie* (Leipzig: Klinkhardt, 1911).

Dahl, Robert A. *Who Governs? Democracy and Power in an American City*. New Haven, CT: Yale University Press, 1961.

Pareto, Vilfredo. *The Mind and Society: A Treatise on General Sociology*. Translated by Andrew Bongiorno and Arthur Livingston. 4 vols. New York: Harcourt, Brace and Co., 1935. Originally published as *Trattato di sociologia generale* (1916).

Schmitt, Carl. *The Concept of the Political*. Translated by George Schwab. Expanded edition. Chicago: University of Chicago Press, 2007. Originally published as *Der Begriff des Politischen* (Berlin: Duncker & Humblot, 1932).

Gambetta, Diego. *The Sicilian Mafia: The Business of Private Protection*. Cambridge, MA: Harvard University Press, 1993.

Organised Crime, Informal Sovereignty, and Political Sociology

Ferguson, Niall. *The Great Degeneration: How Institutions Decay and Economies Die*. New York: Penguin Press, 2012.

Bourdieu, Pierre. *On the State: Lectures at the Collège de France, 1989–1992*. Edited by Patrick Champagne et al. Translated by David Fernbach. Cambridge: Polity Press, 2014.

Bayat, Asef. *Life as Politics: How Ordinary People Change the Middle East*. Stanford, CA: Stanford University Press, 2010.

Fukuyama, Francis. *The Origins of Political Order: From Prehuman Times to the French Revolution*. New York: Farrar, Straus and Giroux, 2011.

Sahlins, Marshall. *Stone Age Economics.* Chicago: Aldine-Atherton, 1972.

Tilly, Charles. *Coercion, Capital, and European States, AD 990–1992.* Revised edition. Cambridge, MA: Blackwell, 1992.

Franchetti, Leopoldo. *Sicily: Its Political and Social Institutions.* Translated by J. D. Meiklejohn. London: Longmans, Green, and Co., 1876.

Friedrichs, David O. *Trusted Criminals: White Collar Crime in Contemporary Society.* 3rd ed. Belmont, CA: Thomson Wadsworth, 2007.

Supplementary Theoretical Texts on Political Sociology

Simmel, Georg. *Conflict and the Web of Group Affiliations.* Translated by Kurt H. Wolff and Reinhard Bendix. New York: Free Press, 1955. Originally published as *Der Streit* in *Soziologie* (1908).

Weber, Max. *Economy and Society: An Outline of Interpretive Sociology.* Edited by Guenther Roth and Claus Wittich. Translated by Ephraim Fischoff et al. Berkeley: University of California Press, 1978. Originally published posthumously in German in 1922.

Huntington, Samuel P. *The Third Wave: Democratization in the Late Twentieth Century.* Norman: University of Oklahoma Press, 1991.

Index of Persons

Amari, Michele

(1806–1889) Sicilian historian, politician, and orientalist. He wrote a history of the 13th-century Sicilian Vespers revolt and served as Minister of Education after Italian unification. Associated with liberal nationalism, Amari is cited in the text to signal the distinguished heritage of the Kalsa district.

Arcos, Count of

Spanish viceroy of Naples during Masaniello's revolt. He orchestrated the downfall of the Neapolitan leader by inciting factionalism and manipulating social unrest. A historical analogue to Los Vélez in Sicily.

Beccaria, Monsignor

A priest who appears in a contemporary anecdote involving the final hours of Antonio di Rudinì. He attempted to offer last rites to the dying former Prime Minister and is described as a family friend. His presence underscores Rudinì's respect for religion despite not being a practicing Catholic.

Consuls of the Guilds, the

Elected heads of Sicily's artisan guilds, they held judicial and administrative authority within their trades. In cities like Palermo, they were part of the civic power structure, serving as local magistrates, city defenders, and intermediaries between the people and municipal government.

Crispi, Francesco

Italian statesman and revolutionary (1818–1901), born in Sicily. Initially a supporter of Garibaldi, Crispi became a central figure in Italian unification and later Prime Minister. A proponent of colonial expansion and centralised authority, he fell from power after scandals and the 1896 defeat at Adwa. Often contrasted with Rudinì for his aggressive, authoritarian style.

D'Alessi, Giuseppe

A Sicilian goldsmith turned revolutionary, D'Alessi led a short-lived popular uprising in Palermo in 1647, inspired by Masaniello's revolt in Naples. Backed by artisan guilds, he expelled the Spanish viceroy and briefly instituted radical democratic reforms. Like his Neapolitan counterpart, he was killed within a week by rival factions. His death ended the reform movement he initiated.

Deputazione del Regno, the

A permanent commission of the Sicilian Parliament responsible for monitoring public spending and safeguarding legal limits on executive power. It served as a key institutional check during the Spanish and early Bourbon eras, emblematic of Sicily's once-robust constitutional autonomy.

Di Blasi (Giovanni Evangelista Di Blasi)

An 18th-century Sicilian historian who documented Palermo's municipal systems and food policies. Cited for his observations on famine, grain supply, and popular unrest, Di Blasi provides a crucial source for understanding early modern Sicilian civic life. He died in the early 19th century, having lived through the major economic and social crises he described.

Einaudi, Luigi

Italian economist and later President of Italy (1948–1955). As an economist, Einaudi studied agrarian economics and property systems. Cited for his work on land use in Italy, including observations on the relationship between agricultural practices and land ownership structures, especially in Sicily and Piedmont.

Ferrara, Giuseppe

Likely referring to a 19th-century literary or civic figure from Palermo, but no prominent national biography exists under this name matching the timeframe. He is briefly mentioned as a notable from the Kalsa district alongside Meli and Amari, likely representing the intellectual prestige of that neighbourhood.

Fusella, Ambrogio

A fictional character from *The Betrothed* (*I Promessi Sposi*) by Alessandro Manzoni. A shady swordsman, Fusella proposes a cynical bread-rationing scheme to protagonist Renzo. He is invoked in the Sicilian context as a literary parallel to cynical or manipulative municipal policy during famine.

Gaetani, Cesare, Prince of Cassero

A Sicilian noble and praetor of Palermo during the 1773 food crisis. He attempted to reform and rescue the failing municipal grain distribution system by pledging his personal fortune. Admired for his integrity and popularity, Gaetani died shortly after taking office, sparking rumours of poisoning and triggering mass riots that ultimately led to the expulsion of the Viceroy.

Galantuomini, the

Literally "gentlemen," this term referred to the rural bourgeoisie in Sicily, especially in interior towns. Typically landowners or professionals of modest means, they formed the political elite in small municipalities. Though distinct from the nobility, they held significant social and administrative power, often through clubs and patronage networks.

Giolitti, Giovanni

Italy's most influential Prime Minister in the early 20th century (served five terms between 1892 and 1921). Known for his flexible, centrist governance and for balancing repression and reform. He distanced himself from Crispi and Rudinì's more authoritarian approaches. Giolitti's government oversaw social reforms and managed the early labour movements, though critics accused him of tolerating corruption.

Honourable Guilds (Arti onorate), the

Artisan and trade guilds in cities like Palermo, which wielded both military and political clout. They defended city walls, administered justice within their trades, and played major roles in uprisings and civic governance. Their militancy and organisation made them a political force into the 18th century.

Le Bon, Gustave

A French social psychologist (1841–1931) known for his theories on crowd psychology and mass behaviour. Cited in the text to support the claim that southern Italian beliefs (e.g. in state poisoning during epidemics) reflect deeply ingrained historical mindsets shaped over centuries.

Los Vélez, Marquis of

Spanish viceroy of Sicily during the 1647 Palermo uprising.

He enforced harsh tax increases and grain reforms during a famine, sparking rebellion. After fleeing the city, he died two months after the uprising. Historian La Lumia called him a "pompous nonentity" ill-equipped for his role.

Masaniello (Tommaso Aniello)

A Neapolitan fishmonger who led a famed revolt in 1647 against Spanish rule in Naples due to rising food prices and taxation. Though initially hailed as a people's leader, he was murdered after days in power. His insurrection became a model for popular uprisings in early modern Italy.

Meli, Giovanni

(1740–1815) A celebrated Sicilian poet and physician from Palermo, known for his lyrical poems written in the Sicilian dialect. His work idealised rural life and local culture. He is cited in the text as a native of the Kalsa district, used to contrast with the Albergheria neighbourhood's later association with political populism.

Miceli

Likely refers to a Palermo police informant or political figure murdered in connection with mafia-linked reprisals in the late 19th century. Mentioned alongside Notarbartolo as a possible victim of political crime. The identity is less documented than Notarbartolo but tied to the broader trial involving Raffaele Palizzolo.

Nasi, Nunzio

A Sicilian politician and Minister of Public Education (1898–1903), Nasi was convicted of embezzlement by Italy's High Court. Despite this, he was celebrated in his hometown of Trapani and became a symbol of southern resentment toward northern judgment. Widely believed in Sicily to have been scapegoated for political reasons

Notarbartolo, Emanuele

Former director of the Bank of Sicily and mayor of Palermo, Notarbartolo was assassinated in 1893, likely for exposing corruption in Sicilian banking and politics. His murder became a symbol of mafia infiltration of public institutions. Palizzolo was suspected of ordering the killing, triggering one of Italy's most high-profile political trials.

Ottavio Lanza, Don, Prince of Trabia

A Sicilian noble who played a central role in suppressing D'Alessi's uprising in 1647 by fostering division among rebel factions. His actions illustrate the entrenched power of aristocratic and ecclesiastical elites in undermining populist movements. Palizzolo, Raffaele

A Sicilian politician (b. 1853) and multiple-term deputy for Palermo, Palizzolo rose through patronage, offering favours in exchange for loyalty. He was later accused of involvement in the 1893 assassination of Emanuele Notarbartolo. Though convicted in Bologna (1902), he was acquitted in a retrial in Florence (1904). Seen in the North as a symbol of elite mafia ties, in Palermo he retained a strong popular base.

Pretore and Senate of Palermo, the

The Pretore was Palermo's chief magistrate and executive, assisted by six senators drawn from the nobility (and occasionally the commoners). Together, they governed the commune like a small state within the state, with control over trade, policing, and public services like the grain supply.

Pro-Palizzolo Committee, the

An informal group in Palermo formed after Palizzolo's 1904 acquittal, aimed at rehabilitating his image and returning him to political office. Though presented as a grassroots movement, it was backed by networks of favour-trading, and its activities were viewed with alarm by critics of corruption and mafia influence.

Rudinì, Antonio di

Sicilian noble and Italian Prime Minister (1891–1892, 1896–1898). He began as a revolutionary against the Bourbons and served as mayor of Palermo, quelling the 1866 uprising. As Prime Minister, he sought fiscal consolidation and peace in Africa after the Adwa disaster. Though accused of weakness during the 1898 bread riots, he remained a respected statesman until his death in 1908.

Tanucci, Bernardo

An influential statesman and reformer from Tuscany who served as Minister and then de facto Prime Minister of the Kingdom of Naples under Charles III and later Ferdinand IV. Known for his anticlerical stance and Enlightenment reforms, Tanucci is cited as a key figure supporting Viceroy Fogliani's long tenure in Sicily.

Trivulzio, Cardinal Teodoro

A Milanese noble and former warrior who became viceroy of Sicily after the 1647 revolt. He implemented modest economic reforms and appealed to popular demands with promises of "bread, justice, and renewal," gaining support among artisan classes during a time of deep economic crisis.

Viceroy's Camarilla, the

An informal group of courtiers, flatterers, and power-seekers who surrounded long-serving viceroys like Fogliani. Their access to power often enabled corruption and clientelism. In the absence of rotation, as with Fogliani's 18-year tenure, this group became a focal point of resentment and popular rebellion.

Villabianca (Marchese di Villabianca)

A Sicilian nobleman and chronicler of 18th-century Palermo. Known for his critical and sarcastic tone, he offers an insider's view of the political and social elite. He provided key historical accounts contrasting official narratives, often highlighting bureaucratic failures and abuses of power.

Index

Other Books by Imperium Press

W. E. Hearn	The Indo-European Household
Wilhelm Roscher	Caesarism
Numa Fustel de Coulanges	The Ancient City (Traditional Histories series)
Neema Parvini	The Populist Delusion
Georges Sorel	Reflections on Violence
Edgar Julius Jung	On the Threshold of a New Era (Studies in Reaction series)
Karl Kudwig von Haller	Restoration of Political Science
J. D. Unwin	Sex and Culture
Yamamoto Tsunetomo	Hagakure
John W. Burgess	The Foundations of Political Science
Mike Maxwell	The Cultured Thug Handbook
John C. Calhoun	A Disquisition on Government (Studies in Reaction series)
Arthur Moeller van den Bruck	The Right of the Young Peoples

www.imperiumpress.org

Printed in Dunstable, United Kingdom

71031374R10123